Better Letters

A Handbook of Business & Personal Correspondence

Jan Venolia

Author of Write Right!

Ten Speed Press 10 / Periwinkle Press

1❿

Ten Speed Press
PO Box 7123
Berkeley, California 94707

Library of Congress Catalogue Number 82-80209
ISBN 0-89815-064-7 (paperbound)
ISBN 0-89815-066-3 (spiralbound)
ISBN 0-89815-065-5 (clothbound)

Cover Design by Brenton Beck
Book Design by Beverly Anderson Graphic Design
Type set by Green Mountain Graphics
Printed in the United States of America

10 9 8 7 6 5 4 3 2 1

Business, love, and friendship
all demand a ready pen.
— The New Universal Letter-Writer,
1850

   . . . or typewriter,
      . . . or word processor

Jan Venolia

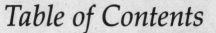

Table of Contents

For centuries, letters have been indispensable in doing business and keeping in touch with friends. But in recent years our methods of writing them have changed dramatically. We have gone from manual to electric typewriters, from self-correcting typewriters to word processors; each advance has introduced new levels of speed and economy. Letters are now made in an instant—copy after copy, without a single typo. They can be whisked around the globe electronically, completely bypassing the post office.

But while we have concentrated on the speed of producing our letters, we have often ignored their quality. Companies invest in sophisticated equipment, only to churn out hundreds of letters that lack any spark of originality. Even the name *word processor* is suggestive: we no longer write messages, we process words. You can almost hear the machinery clanking.

Better Letters is written on the premise that *what* you write is important; that in the rush to automate, you should not lose sight of the end product—your letter—and its potential impact on your reader.

Robert Louis Stevenson stated the case succinctly:

> *The difficulty is not to write, but to write what you mean; not to affect your reader, but to affect him precisely as you wish.*

Writing well takes careful thinking about why you are writing, and then organizing words to achieve your goal. If you turn to letter-writing handbooks for help, you will find that most are badly out of date. Many consist of model letters "for every occasion." An ingenious variety is presented for your use, but how many of us need to write to an undertaker, or to decline an invitation to judge a dog show? You are told to change a word here and there to make the models fit your own requirements, "without wasting valuable time and effort." I can hear the machinery clanking again . . . visions of model letters, slightly modified but always off target, shuttling back and forth between word processors.

Can *any* model letter express your ideas and affect your reader precisely as you wish? *Better Letters* assumes that the writer, who knows best why he or she is writing, can produce a letter superior to any modified model. Irrelevant examples and obsolete advice will not help. Today's letter writer needs an up-to-date handbook that covers the essentials and is easy to use. I hope this is such a book.

Skim through the pages to acquaint yourself with their contents. Chapter 1 *(Letter Writing Style)* is a quick course in the elements of good writing; Chapter 2 *(Composing a Better Letter)* applies the rules of style to letter writing; Chapter 3 *(Format)* presents options for making your letters eye-appealing and correct by modern standards. Chapters 4 *(Business Letters)* and 5 *(Personal Letters)* contain advice about specific types of business and personal correspondence; some samples are included to spark ideas about how to write your own letters.

Chapter 6 *(Dear Sir or Madam)* is devoted to the subject of nonsexist writing — a topic that most handbooks either ignore or try to deal with in just a few sentences. Chapter 7 *(The Benevolent Dictator)* will help if you are just starting to dictate letters or if you want to polish your dictating technique.

Better Letters is the logical outgrowth of my first book, *Write Right! A Desk Drawer Digest of Punctuation, Grammar & Style. Write Right!* focuses on such problems as spelling, usage, where to put commas and apostrophes, and so on. As a companion volume, *Better Letters* emphasizes style, format, and the specifics of letter writing.

Knowing how to write good letters is an asset, in business as well as in personal matters. *Better Letters* gives you the tools you need for the job. When so much human contact has been replaced by digits and plastic cards, a letter written with care and intelligence is likely to produce a favorable response. In a world where slapdash compromise is much too common, your well-crafted letter will be a standout.

1
Letter Writing Style

CHAPTER 1
Letter-Writing Style

Letter writing is a special kind of writing, directed to a particular audience for a specific purpose. Your audience may be one person or thousands of people. Your reason for writing may be critically important to your business, or it may be the desire to keep in touch with friends. Whatever the nature of your letter, you should make it *clear*, *concise*, and *readable*.

Write Clearly

The task of clear writing has two main components:
Choosing the best words to express your ideas,
Arranging the words to help the reader grasp your ideas.

Words are your tools. The more words you have at your command, the more accurately they can convey your ideas. The more effectively you arrange them, the more successful you will be in moving an idea from your mind to your reader's.

> *A word is not a crystal, transparent and unchanged; it is the skin of a living thought and may vary greatly in color and content according to the circumstances and time in which it is used.* — Oliver Wendell Holmes, Jr.

Have a dictionary nearby when you write. It can help you in many ways:

- with spelling (supersede or supercede?)
- with word division (know-ledge or knowl-edge?)
- with definitions (what does "colloquial" mean?)
- with usage (is *typo* colloquial?)
- with plurals (memorandums or memoranda?)
- with synonyms (burn, scorch, or singe?)
- with pronunciation (kewlinary or kullinary?)
- with word roots (polyglot: from Greek *poly* [much, many] + *glotta* [tongue])

Use fresh words.

Writers of letters are often told to write the way they speak. Anyone who has transcribed a conversation can see the problem in taking this suggestion literally. Our speech is full of redundancies, false starts, disjointed delivery, and extra words. We punctuate sentences with "you know" and often rely on gestures and facial expressions to carry our meaning.

But the write-as-you-speak rule does contain a kernel of truth: You don't speak stilted language, so why write it? The words you put on the page should be ones you can imagine yourself saying. Following this principle will eliminate such sentences as:

"Receipt of yours of August 22 is acknowledged herewith."

Would you ever say that to anyone? Or how about:

"With reference to your recent inquiry regarding the availability of . . . , please be advised that due to the fact that Blank Company no longer manufactures . . . , the above-referenced items have been removed from our product line as of the present writing. Thanking you for your interest, I remain, . . ."

When writing business letters, people often use jargon they wouldn't think of putting in a personal letter. Unfortunately, this situation seems to be self-perpetuating. One jargon-filled letter begets another when we use the incoming mail as our standard.

Ready-made phrases are the prefabricated strips of words . . . that come crowding in when you do not want to take the trouble to think through what you are saying. They will construct your sentences for you — even think your thoughts for you . . . — and at need they will perform the important service of partially concealing your meaning even from yourself. — George Orwell

The best way to cut through jargon is to edit ruthlessly. Challenge each sentence with the question "Is there a simpler way to say that?" If a group of words occurs to you automatically, chances are that you should reach a little farther for a less hackneyed phrase. Be on the lookout for today's buzz words:

finalize	input	parameter	at this point in time
impact	interface	taxwise	bite the bullet
implement	net net	viable	bottom line

Writing that is heavy with words such as these suggests parroted formulas instead of original thought.

The following letter is composed almost entirely of stilted and redundant phrases.

> With reference to your letter of March 21, which we acknowledge receipt of herewith, we would like to take this opportunity to make inquiry regarding your payment in the amount of $150 as per our agreement and which according to our records we are not in receipt of despite the fact that we called same to your attention in the recent past with a view to availing you of the opportunity at your earliest convenience to correct this oversight. Until such time as you are prepared to make payment, we are not in a position, with all due regard, to continue to extend credit in this connection and beg to advise you to give this matter your utmost attention without further delay.

What this letter really says is:

> Until we receive payment of the $150 you owe us, we can no longer extend credit to you.

A tongue-in-cheek approach to the same problem might read:

> If you don't pay the $150 you owe us, I will tell your other creditors you did.

Words that impart a legal flavor are especially overworked—and usually inappropriate. Unless you are a lawyer, avoid expressing yourself with such words as the following:

aforementioned	notwithstanding the above
duly	per, as per
herein	pursuant to
hereto	re
herewith	therein

Even if you *are* a lawyer, you can find better ways to express yourself.

Use concrete words.

Concrete words are specific. They deal with things we can see, hear, smell, touch, and taste; things we know firsthand, like razors, Boston cream pie, petunias, hangnails, hot tubs, and disc jockeys.

Abstract words have different meanings for different people—liberty, hunger, danger, speed, heroism. When you write in abstractions and generalities, you place upon your reader the burden of trying to figure out what you mean. Vagueness may be tempting since it usually takes less effort. But if you wish to convert a flabby style into a crisp one, if you wish to arouse and hold your reader's interest, you will deal in particulars and your language will be specific, definite, and concrete.

Charles Dickens' character Mr. Macawber provides an example of both an overblown abstraction and its concrete translation:

> *It is not an avocation of a remunerative description—in other words, it does not pay.*

The following examples illustrate how to turn a vague statement into a more precise one.

(Vague)   Mrs. Halliday is a hard worker.

(Precise)   Mrs. Halliday often devotes part of her lunch hour to getting an important letter ready to mail.

(Vague)	Our primary objective is to consider available alternatives in order to determine a viable option for improving working conditions by removing environmental hazards.
(Precise)	We want to find a way to remove airborne asbestos particles.

(Vague)	In view of our domestic economic situation . . .
(Precise)	With unemployment near seven percent . . .

(Vague)	We experienced a marked increase in productivity after management introduced a program to improve the health of our employees.
(Precise)	The exercise and nutrition program cut absenteeism in half.

Rather than referring to "optimum test results" or "adverse weather conditions," say what the results or conditions are. Your readers will respond more quickly to "35 miles per gallon" or "a temperature of 25 degrees below zero."

Here is a pair of quotations with similar meanings; the second writer has brought the idea to life with her specific example.

> *The average man, who does not know what to do with his life, wants another one which will last forever.* — Anatole France

> *Millions long for immortality who do not know what to do with themselves on a rainy Sunday afternoon.* — Susan Ertz

Verbs such as *exist, happen, occur,* and *take place* often produce vague, colorless sentences.

Weak:	During the strike, tension existed between management and labor.
Stronger:	During the strike, tension between management and labor grew.

Weak:	A sharp drop occurred in the Dow Jones Industrial Average.
Stronger:	The Dow Jones Industrial Average dropped sharply.

Generalities have their function. They provide the framework for organizing information into ideas and summaries. But when you have climbed into the stratosphere to state a lofty principle, scurry back to sea level with a tangible example as quickly as you can.

Make concrete words carry your abstract idea. Writing a letter that clearly conveys your meaning costs less than writing a letter which is so ambiguous that further correspondence is needed.

Use short, familiar words.

> ... *except ye utter by the tongue words easy to be understood, how shall it be known what is spoken?*—I Corinthians 14:9

Vivid words tend to be short ones, like those we use in everyday speech. When your words are familiar to your reader, you improve the odds that your letter will be understood. Choose words like *begin, move,* and *use* rather than *initiate, relocate,* and *utilize.*

Gelett Burgess (of Purple Cow fame) wrote an eight-page essay of one-syllable words. Here is an excerpt:

> If we use long words too much, we are apt to talk in ruts and use the same old, worn ways of speech .... Short words are bold. They say just what they mean. They do not leave you in doubt. They are clear and sharp, like signs cut in rock.

Use the right words.

Know when to write *definite* and when to write *definitive*. Avoid confusing *affect* with *effect, principal* with *principle, disinterested* with *uninterested.*

Here are some commonly misused pairs of words:

Affect is a verb meaning to have an influence on; *effect* is both a noun (meaning result or consequence) and a verb (meaning to bring about).
> New employees are not affected by the ruling.
> The effect of the ruling is limited.
> Management has effected new procedures.

Alternate refers to every other one; *alternative* is a choice.
> One alternative is to meet on alternate Tuesdays.

Complement means to complete a whole or satisfy a need; *compliment* means praise.

> Their efforts were complementary.
>
> The group leader complimented them on their teamwork.

Continual means over and over again; *continuous* means uninterrupted or unbroken.

> Since he coughed continually, the doctor kept him under continuous observation.

Definite usually means clear-cut, unequivocal; *definitive* means complete and authoritative.

> I will give you a definite answer next week.
>
> She has written the definitive treatment of the subject.

Disinterested means objective or neutral; *uninterested* means lacking interest.

> A disinterested third party is needed.
>
> He was uninterested in the results.

Fewer is used for number, especially when referring to individual numbers or units; *less* is used for quantity, as in periods of time, sums of money, or measures of weight or distance.

> Automation requires more machines and fewer people.
>
> Her salary was less than his.

Using words such as these incorrectly suggests sloppy thinking and generally careless work. *Write Right!* contains a longer list of abused words to help you sort them out.

Make your references clear.

Many words refer to or modify other words. If your readers don't know which words you are referring to or modifying, they may fail to follow your line of thought. You may even provide them with a loud guffaw if you juxtapose words ineptly.

> The president of the company is a distinguished-looking gentleman with a well-trimmed beard named Marshall Myers.

> If you do not have a vehicle in which to store your food,

please do not hesitate to ask for assistance in properly hanging it from a Park Ranger.

Keep modifiers as close as possible to the words you are modifying. Rewrite:

> We will be interviewing during the coming weeks before summer vacation, individuals who are qualified to serve as playground directors.

to read:

> Before summer vacation, we will be interviewing individuals who are qualified to serve as playground directors.

Place adverbs so the reader knows which word they modify. A sentence like the following may force the reader to go over it twice to determine whether *recently* modifies *received* or *managed*.

| (Poor) | A letter I received recently managed to irritate the entire family. |
| (Better) | Recently I received a letter that managed to irritate the entire family. |

Be especially careful about placement of the adverb *only*. Meaning is distorted if *only* does not precede the word it is supposed to modify. For example:

> The computer can only accept four drives.

The order of those words suggests that the only function the computer can perform is to accept four drives. Moving *only* so that it follows *accept* makes the intended meaning clear.

> The computer can accept only four drives.

Keep subject and verb together to help the reader.

| (Poor) | Members of the Board of Directors, who are elected by district each November to serve four-year staggered terms and whose duties require attendance at only one meeting per week, are not eligible for pensions under the city charter. |

Often the information that separates subject and verb belongs in a second sentence.

| (Better) | Members of the Board of Directors are elected by district each November to serve four-year staggered terms. |

Since they are only required to attend one meeting per week, they are not eligible for pensions under the city charter.

Make sure your references are correct. Words like *who, which, that,* and *it* refer to the preceding noun; if the preceding noun is not the word you intend to refer to, or if too many words stand between the noun and its referent, you must rewrite. Incorrect references can mislead or confuse. They can also be unintentionally humorous. For example:

This is the last year for the 55% Solar Tax Credit for pools. Solar heat your pool now before it expires.

The intended meaning of this advertising copy is clear, but the picture of a pool expiring tickles my imagination. In a sentence such as the following, however, the meaning is not clear. I've counted six interpretations of it; how many can you find?

Elaine told Diane's sister that she must pay her.

Just what is being referred to in the following sentences?

(1) The senator proposed an amendment of the administration tax bill, *which* was opposed by the steel manufacturers.

Was the amendment or the tax bill opposed?

(2) The wife of my partner, *who* died recently . . .

Who died, the wife or the partner?

(3) The information contained in this report, *which* has not been available previously because of proprietary concern, remains confidential and should be filed in a secure place.

Was the report or the information proprietary?

(4) The stockholders alleged fraud and mismanagement in the handling of corporate funds, dating back to when *it* was run by . . .

What does *it* refer to? *The corporation,* which does not appear as such in the sentence.

Rewrite those sentences to remove sloppy references, using the following techniques.

Rearrange words:

(1) The steel manufacturers opposed the senator's amendment of the administration tax bill.

(2) My partner's wife died recently.

Form two sentences:

(3) This confidential report contains proprietary information which was not previously available. Please file the report in a secure place.

Avoid vague pronouns:

(4) The stockholders alleged fraud and mismanagement in the handling of corporate funds, dating back to when the corporation was run by . . .

In some cases, a pronoun refers correctly to an antecedent but nonetheless provides a laugh.

If the children do not like raw vegetables, boil them.

Avoid this type of situation by rewriting.

Write Concisely

The most valuable of all talents is that of never using two words when one will do. —Thomas Jefferson

Strike out unnecessary words.

If this one dictum were observed, the quality and effectiveness of most writing would be dramatically improved. Many of our habitual expressions violate this principle. We use not just two but several words where one would do.

> Some questions relating to this issue . . .
> Some relevant questions . . .

We use roundabout instead of direct wording.

> in view of the fact that
> owing to the fact that   = because
> due to the fact that
>
> in spite of the fact that   = although
>
> The fact that we arrived late . . .   = Our late arrival . . .

Here are some typical ways we pad our writing, followed by leaner versions of each.

> During the course of the campaign . . .
> During the campaign . . .
>
> Our marketing staff is now engaged in a study . . .
> Our marketing staff is now studying . . .
>
> In about a month's time . . .
> In about a month . . .
>
> A new car quickly depreciates in value.
> A new car depreciates quickly.
>
> . . . on a theoretical level
> . . . in theory
>
> The reason I like the book is that . . .
> I like the book because . . .

We often pad sentences in order to make them appear more polite or dignified. Empty phrases such as *You can appreciate that, consideration should be given to, it is a matter of prime importance, for your information,* or *in this connection* contribute nothing to the reader's understanding of your meaning. Eliminate them.

Rewrite most sentences to avoid the phrases *there is* and *there are.*
> There are several companies that are qualified to do the work.
> Several companies are qualified to do the work.

> Throughout the day, there was an atmosphere of increasing excitement.
> Throughout the day, excitement mounted.

Drop *that* unless meaning requires it.
> I think that the book that she wants is that one.
Only the last *that* is essential to the meaning.

Clauses beginning with *which, that,* or *who* can frequently be compressed into fewer words.
> The senator, who comes from Ohio, gave a speech that was long and tedious.
> The Senator from Ohio gave a long, tedious speech.

> The board meeting, which lasted two hours, was followed by a press conference.
> The two-hour board meeting was followed by a press conference. *or*
> A press conference followed the two-hour board meeting.

Omission of the article *the* often improves the readability of a sentence.
> The proposed improvements will eliminate ~~the~~ outside timesharing.

> The characteristics of ~~the~~ future systems will not require ...

> ~~The~~ determination of maintenance time requirements, ~~the~~ design criteria to accomplish them, and ~~the~~ verification that the design is adequate are elements of the program.

Perhaps the best way to determine if *the* is needed is to try omitting it. You will quickly discover which ones are essential for clarity and style.

The following list suggests alternatives for some common wordy—
and frequently incorrect—expressions. Your readers will appreciate
the vigor and directness of your writing if you use the shorter, simpler
words.

Replace:	with:
and etc.	etc.
at all times	always
at that point in time	then
at this point in time	now
conclusive proof	proof
consensus of opinion	consensus
deeds and actions	(Use one or the other)
during the course of	during
exactly identical	identical
exact same	(Use one or the other)
few in number	few
first and foremost	(Use one or the other)
for the period of a year	for a year
have a belief in	believe
if and when	(Use one or the other)
in the vast majority of cases	in most cases
my personal opinion	my opinion *or* I believe that
on a monthly basis	monthly
positive identification	identification
blue in color	blue
reduce to a minimum	minimize
refer back to	refer to
reiterate again	reiterate
round in shape	round
streamlined in appearance	streamlined
true facts	facts
unless and until	(Use one or the other)
until such time as	until
various different	(Use one or the other)
very necessary	necessary
(relevant, true)	(relevant, true)

Use adjectives and adverbs sparingly.

When you use modifiers, make them work for you. Vigorous adjectives and adverbs add to your meaning.

local monopoly	baffling instructions
crisp dialogue	sweaty palms
jovial manner	crabbed style

Overused modifiers, on the other hand, give your writing the stale flavor of cliches.

richly deserved	absolute necessity
eminently qualified	bitter end
perfectly clear	checkered career
acid test	final analysis

When you feel the need to prop up a word with an adjective or adverb, consider whether the word by itself might be stronger.

(Poor)   His response was quick and very emphatic.
(Better)   His response was quick and emphatic.

Keep your sentences short.

Short sentences are characteristic of good modern writing. Today's average sentence of 20 words contrasts with the 60 words of a few centuries ago. Experts insist that short sentences are more understandable, and evidence indicates that readers prefer them.

Long sentences usually result from our failure to *think* before writing. We plunge into a sentence with an idea and then stumble along, adding exceptions, qualifiers, and incidental remarks. We create a verbal maze for our readers.

Perhaps the problem stems from our concern that each sentence must express a complete thought. As soon as we state an idea, we realize that it isn't complete without some background information or qualifying remarks; or our original idea branches in several directions. Our "complete thought" becomes bogged down by its own weight.

Coherence may be a better criterion in shaping sentences. Let the words between two periods express a unified idea—but not everything there is to say about a given subject.

A sentence such as the following has several ideas embedded in it and should be rewritten as two sentences.

(Poor)   Today we shipped your order of January 10 by express freight, and you should be receiving it within a few days, but since you are a new customer I wanted you to know that we allow an additional discount of 3% if we receive your payment before the end of the month.

The conjunctions *and* and *but* are sometimes signals that a new sentence is needed. A series of independent clauses connected by *and* and *but* leaves the reader feeling dragged along. Here is one way to rewrite the example above:

(Better)   Your order of January 10 was shipped today by express freight and should arrive in a few days. As a new customer, you may not be aware that we allow an additional 3% discount for payment received before the end of the month.

A sentence should read as if its author, had he held a plough instead of a pen, could have drawn a furrow deep and straight to the end. — Thoreau

---

Sometimes you have to rewrite one sentence as several to make it more manageable.

(Poor)   I am sorry to report that because of a severe winter storm that closed our factory and disrupted delivery of two critical components your shipment will be two weeks late, but we have now received all the necessary parts and our crew is working overtime to put production back on schedule.

(Better)   I am sorry to report that your shipment will be two weeks late. A winter storm that closed our factory disrupted delivery of two critical components. However, we now have all the necessary parts, and our crew is working overtime to put production back on schedule.

Write with a Readable Style

Writing with a readable style shows that you are aware of the person reading your letter. It acknowledges your desire to engage the reader's attention and interest. By observing a few rules, you can improve the readability of your writing.

Write in the active voice.

When you write in the active voice, the subject of the sentence performs the action:
> Man bites dog.
> The committee read your report.

When you use the passive voice, the subject receives the action.
> Dog bitten by man.
> Your report was read by the committee.

The active voice is more forceful and direct—and often uses fewer words. The passive voice tends to encourage anonymity; reports are written, actions are taken, and suggestions are made in a nameless void.

The passive voice combines a form of the verb *to be* with a past participle: *was read, have been sold, were reported, had been opened, will have been seen.* Become expert at sniffing out passive constructions and converting them to the active form.

Passive: A feasibility study was conducted by the marketing staff.
Active: The marketing staff conducted a feasibility study.

Passive: Revisions of the charter have been made to remove outdated provisions.
Active: We have revised the charter to remove outdated provisions.

The following sentence shifts from active to passive:
> When the sales representatives completed their reports, the data were analyzed and a marketing plan was outlined by the head of each department.

Here it is, rewritten entirely in the active voice:
> When the sales representatives completed their reports, the head of each department analyzed the data and outlined a marketing plan.

Passive voice is appropriate when the recipient of the action is more important than the performer of the action.

The pedestrian was struck by a car.

The records were lost by a careless employee.

Do not use the passive voice to avoid saying "I" or "we."

(Poor)   It is recommended by this office . . .

(Better)   We recommend . . .

Emphasize important points.

Put more important ideas in the main clause of a sentence, and less important details in subordinate clauses or phrases. For example:

> In view of the large number of books shipped to your company each week, I believe you will be interested in our new volume discount policy.

The main clause, "I believe you will be interested in our new volume discount policy," carries the main idea. The remaining information, even though it appears at the beginning of the sentence, merely buttresses this central point; it is appropriately given less emphasis by being placed in a subordinate clause.

Build to a climax by moving from simple to complicated, least important to most important, and so on.

> The firestorm destroyed trees, homes—entire blocks.

> *I dislike arguments of any kind. They are always vulgar, and often convincing.*—Oscar Wilde

Don't bury your climax in the middle of the sentence.

(Weak)   Our investment in research has finally led to a cure for the common cold, after years of experimentation and unproductive effort.

(Stronger)   After years of tracking down promising leads only to find ourselves in blind alleys, our research has finally paid off with a cure for the common cold.

Inverting the customary order is another way to achieve emphasis.

Right you are!

Behind every successful man stands a surprised mother-in-law.

Itemizing often emphasizes what you want to bring to the reader's attention. Information presented in a list is easier to grasp than the same information in one unbroken paragraph.

(Poor)   To complete your application, we will need to know your address and telephone number, date and place of birth, social security number, current employer, and the name and phone number of three credit references.

(Better)   To complete your application, we will need the following information:
              1. address
              2. telephone number
              3. date of birth
              4. place of birth
              5. social security number
              6. current employer
              7. three credit references (name and phone number)

When itemizing, use a parallel form for each item; that is, if the first item is a complete sentence, make all other items complete sentences; if the first item begins with an infinitive, begin all items with an infinitive. Don't mix phrases, sentences, commands, and nouns in one list.

Wrong: Right:
1. Bring your camera.   1. Bring your camera and a supply
2. A supply of film.   of film.
3. Wear sunglasses.   2. Wear sunglasses.
4. Being on time is important.   3. Be on time.

Avoid monotonous sentences.

Keep your reader's attention by introducing variety in your sentence patterns. A series of short, primer-style sentences lacks interest; furthermore, it gives equal weight to every detail and thus suggests that you have not evaluated your ideas.

Thank you for your letter of March 9. We had never heard of the problem you described. Our production department is looking into it. They will report their findings within a week. We are confident they will find a solution. We will advise you of our findings as soon as they are available. We appreciate your telling us about the problem.

Long, complicated sentence after long, complicated sentence can be equally tedious for the reader.

Thank you for your letter of March 9 in which you describe a type of problem we had never encountered before and which we are grateful for your having brought to our attention. Our production department is seeking a solution, which we are confident they will find, and we will report the results of their research within a week. As soon as we have their report we will notify you of their findings in the hope that their solution will apply to your situation.

Soften the abrupt sentences of the first example by adding introductory phrases and sorting some of the ideas into more-important, less-important clauses. Provide relief from the long-winded sentences in the second example by breaking some of them into smaller units. The result might be something like the following:

The problem you described in your letter of March 9 is one we have never encountered. As soon as our production department finds a solution—probably within a week— we will notify you. We appreciate your having taken the time to write us.

Use paragraphing to help the reader.

Solid pages of type are formidable. By grouping sentences into readable units, you can provide spacing that gives the page a more pleasing appearance and makes your ideas more accessible.

No fixed rule for paragraph length exists, but you should avoid the extremes. Very long paragraphs are difficult to follow; a letter made up entirely of short paragraphs has a breathless, hiccuppy effect on the reader.

See your paragraphs not as isolated units but as coordinated parts of the whole, with each paragraph creating a unified impression and contributing to the smooth flow of ideas. This will happen automatically if you are working from a logical outline.

Do not jar the reader by arbitrarily separating two sentences that obviously belong together. Look for natural ways to group sentences. You may break an overly long paragraph in two, but do not combine two small paragraphs if they deal with different subjects.

Although an entire letter may deal with just one subject, it does not follow that the letter must contain only one paragraph. Proper paragraphing allows you to draw attention to certain points and to change the subject; reserve short paragraphs for the points you want to emphasize most.

Make your subject clear.

The reader should be able to tell without difficulty what each paragraph is about. A key sentence at the beginning or end of a paragraph usually suggests the topic. If the topic sentence appears at the beginning of a paragraph, it should lead into the sentences that follow.

> Market research indicates strong community support for construction of a downtown shopping mall. A poll of residents living within three miles of the proposed site showed that 75 percent would patronize businesses located in the new mall. Sixty percent of the owners of commercial enterprises indicated their desire to move to the mall.

If the topic sentence comes at the end of the paragraph, it should summarize the preceding sentences.

> One shareholder proposed that the Board of Directors be prohibited from making charitable contributions with corporate funds. Another asked that the ethnic makeup of the Board be diversified. Altogether, six proposals were presented by the shareholders.

Letters that are clear, concise, and readable will generally follow the rules described in this chapter. But rules are only guides for most situations. Good writing does not require that you always use short words, short sentences, and the active voice. Knowing the rules allows you to use them or break them, not from ignorance, but from knowledge. If you keep in mind the goals of clarity, conciseness, and readability, your letters will have the desired effect on your reader.

2
Composing a Better Letter

CHAPTER 2
Composing a Better Letter

Writing well need not be difficult, but it does require care and attention. Writing good letters poses an additional challenge: Within a limited space you must win the reader's attention and convey your message. Furthermore, your letter must compete with phone calls, appointments, meetings, and other letters to get your reader's attention.

To compete effectively, a letter should be:

Accurate. Good business relationships are built on precise information.

Clear. Clarity will help your reader understand your message.

Friendly. Stress "you" rather than "I." Show that you understand your reader's situation.

Neat. You never get a second chance to make a good first impression.

Brief. Most people are busy; don't waste their time.

Courteous. No letter is so short or so unimportant that you can omit such conventions of courtesy as "thank you" and "please."

Correct. Use words properly; spell and hyphenate them correctly. A dictionary is a must.

Complete. Don't leave loose ends; provide the necessary information in appropriate detail.

Prompt. Answer letters at the earliest opportunity; it will encourage your correspondent to do the same.

I once received a letter that violated many of these principles in the space of three sentences. The letter is shown at the right, edited only to protect the guilty:

• Although the person dictating obviously meant "taking an," substituting the word "your" improves the sentence.

• Two sentences beginning with "however" make the letter read like a broken record. The second "however" contributes nothing and should be omitted.

• The final sentence is a run-on (i.e., two sentences masquerading as one). Removing the unnecessary words ("padding") from the beginning of the sentence solves that problem.

• The signature block is incorrectly spaced; there should be four blank lines between the complimentary close and the typed name and no blank lines between the typed name and "Research Department."

"Gentlemen:" is an out-moded form of address. See Chapter 6.

Wrong words. See note on facing page.

Periwinkle Press
P. O. Box 1305
Woodland Hills, CA 91365

Gentlemen:

Comma missing after "however"

Poor usage. Substitute "because" for "due to the fact that"

Thank you for taken and interest in Publishers Guide, which is now called National Publishers Guide. However at this time we are unable to send any forms or information on National Publishers Guide due to the fact that the 2nd Edition has been completed and sent to be printed. However we will keep this letter on hand, for when we get ready to start our 3rd Edition, we will contact you.

"2nd" should be written out

First part of last sentence is padding. Sentence should begin "When we..."

Awkward. Substitute "has been typeset and sent to the printer"

Delete "get ready"

Sincerely Yours,
Betty Blank
Betty Blank
Research Department

"3rd" should be written out

"Yours" should not be capitalized

Replace the abused word "contact" with "write to"

Allow more space for signature

The following pages suggest ways to tackle the problems of letter writing: organizing information, analyzing your reader, writing opening and closing paragraphs, and revising your written letters.

Organizing Your Thoughts

Work from an outline.

Thinking must precede writing, and an outline forces you to think. Just what do you want to accomplish by writing the letter? How can you best accomplish it? The more care you put into developing and refining an outline, the more readily the letter will flow when you start dictating or writing it.

Some people insist that an outline is unnecessary—that it is better to start writing the actual letter and make changes after seeing a rough draft. In effect, these individuals are creating an elaborate outline, but calling it a rough draft. They revise the draft only after they have spent considerable time on it.

If revisions are made with a word processor, retyping may be a simple procedure. But if the letter must be completely redone on a conventional typewriter, the duplication of effort can be costly. Furthermore, it is easier to revise an outline than a draft—and you are more likely to do it. You can shuffle ideas around more readily before they become embedded in complete sentences within paragraphs. And you will probably be more willing to make necessary changes if you haven't already invested a lot of time in preparing your first draft.

For a simple letter, the outline could be a mental list of subjects to be covered. Or you might want to make some notes in the margin of a letter to be answered to indicate how you want to respond: "Thanks, but no thanks" or "Request formal proposal for ad campaign."

When you are thoroughly familiar with the subject of a letter, just jot down the key words needed to summon up ideas about each topic. For example:

Quality Assurance Program
    some case histories
    reject ratio
    cost (incl. insurance)
    alternatives
    govt. regs.
    recommendations

A brief but slightly more elaborate outline might look like this:

1. Acknowledge customer's request for waiver of late-payment penalty
   - frustration of "first-time offender"
   - record of timely payments

2. Put problem in perspective
   - 10-day grace period allowed
   - exceptions: difficulties created by making them
   - interest rates, inflation, cash flow

3. Sympathetic "no"

As the subject matter or objectives of the letter become more complex, make your outline more detailed.

1. List the general topics to be covered. For the moment assume that each will be a paragraph. Don't worry about their order yet.

2. Under each topic enter key words, examples, or facts that will help you remember what you want to write.

3. Determine the order of the items within each topic and mark them accordingly. Place the more important material at the beginning or end of the paragraph, since those are the spots most easily caught by the reader's eye. Does the reader need certain information in order to understand what follows? If so, be sure to put that information first. Any topic that appears to include too many sub-topics should be broken into more than one paragraph.

4. Review your outline for its relevance to your purpose in sending the letter. Is any of your information trivial? Is there enough evidence to support your conclusions? If necessary, revise your outline to keep yourself on the track.

5. Finally, number the paragraphs according to the order in which you want to present your ideas. Do you want to start the letter with your

central thought or statement and then buttress it with discussion and examination? Or would you prefer to build to a climax by identifying a question or issue, then discussing it, and finally presenting your conclusions? Some subjects lend themselves to a chronological or narrative arrangement in which you discuss events in the order of their occurrence or answer questions in the order they were raised.

Long, important letters almost demand extensive outlining. The following example was written for an in-house memo addressed to ABC Company's sales force:

1. Introduction
   a. long awaited
      – extensive R&D
   b. importance in ABC's product line
   c. timing of entry into new market
2. Description of Gadgetron
   a. dimensions, power requirements, etc.
   b. features/capabilities
         ("user friendly")
   c. prices of basic models, options
         (enclose price list)
3. Market test results
   a. consumer acceptance
   b. competition/competitive edge
4. National advertising campaign
   Timing of:
   a. TV-radio spots
   b. display ads (magazines)
   c. billboards (which cities)
5. Sales incentive program
   a. 4 regional contests
   b. no. of winners
      – description of prizes
   c. additional $ for best promotional idea
6. Closing
   a. reminder to take advantage of natl. publicity for sales of related ABC products (Widgetron, Maxitron)
   b. Ads don't make sales — they just get the customer ready. It's up to us!

```
1. Introduction
     important to ABC Co.
     long-awaited — extensive R+D
     timing of entry
5. Sales Incentive Prog.
     b. prizes, no. winners
     c. Addl. $ for best promo idea
     a. date/place of presentation  4 regional contests
2. Description
     b. features/capabilities ("user friendly")
     a. dimensions, power req.
     c. prices, incl. options*
4. Natl. Ad Campaign
   Media: TV, radio, billboards, mags
     — common unifying theme
     — timing
3. Market Test
   Consumer acceptance of Gadgetron
   Comparison w. competition
     — our competitive edge
6. Closing
     — reminder: use natl. publicity to sell
        related ABC products (such as ?)
     — ads don't make sales — they just get
        cust. ready. It's up to us!
*Enclose price list
```

In the real world, the outline would probably look more like this.

The objective of your letter will probably suggest the best way to organize the flow of information in your paragraphs. Your goal is not to create an impeccable outline that starts with Roman Numeral I and marches down the page with successive tidy indentations. Instead, you want to make sure that you cover everything you want to say and that you do so in the most effective sequence.

Letter Formulas

Some formulas have been created to help identify the elements you should include in a business letter. One such formula lists the essential elements as:

- Occasion (why you're writing)
- Facts (information needed for action)
- Action (may be a request, suggestion, statement or demand)
- Closing (courtesy; an offer of additional help or information)

A popular formula for sales letters is AIDA, an acronym for:

- Attention   (catching the reader's eye)
- Interest   (arousing the reader's interest in what you're writing)
- Desire   (making the reader want what you're selling)
- Action   (showing the reader how to obtain it)

A variation on that theme is:
- Interest
- Desire
- Conviction
- Action

The new element, conviction, refers to the believability of what is presented. Exaggerated claims or failing to present sufficient evidence to back up your statements will damage your credibility.

If you find letter formulas helpful, use them. Before writing, they can help organize your thoughts; after writing, they can serve as a check for completeness or appropriateness of tone. You can probably achieve similar results, however, if you are guided by your goal in writing the letter and your understanding of the best way to achieve that goal.

To write a really first-rate letter requires that you understand what you do and don't know about the reader of the letter. As you gain experience with an individual or a type of clientele, you will sense how to get on the right wavelength.

Analyze Your Reader

Despite the wide variety of personalities we exhibit, human beings tend to be moved by certain common interests:

- Profit (getting more)
- Saving (spending less)
- Health (preserving or improving it)
- Comfort (feeling of well-being)
- Convenience (saving time, increasing efficiency)
- Enjoyment (happiness, personal satisfaction)
- Loyalty (sense of obligation)
- Prestige (pride of ownership, keeping up with the Joneses)

You may want to make up your own list of motivating forces. As you write each letter, show that you understand your reader's problems. What motivates him or her: the need to reduce costs, expand markets, or improve service? How does what you are writing about help? If you want a job, why should the reader consider your qualifications? If you are seeking information, how do you assure the reader's cooperation in providing it? If you want to collect an overdue account, how can you move your reader to pay? How do you establish good will?

You are the one who must provide answers to these questions since you know the pertinent details: the nature of the recipient of the letter, your previous dealings with this person, and so on. But knowing some effective ways to begin and end may help you shape your letter.

Writing the Letter

Opening Paragraphs

Whether you are guided by the AIDA-type formulas described earlier or by common sense, your first job is to engage the reader. A letter that reports a million-dollar inheritance from a remote uncle will have no problem capturing the reader's attention. But most correspondence has less dramatic impact and thus requires some degree of salesmanship. The first paragraph is where that salesmanship begins.

Plunge right into your reason for writing. Abraham Lincoln did so in a letter to his brother-in-law that began this way:

> Your request for eighty dollars, I do not think it best to comply with now.

Don't weigh down the front of your letter with boring repetition of detail that is already known to your correspondent. If you need to refer to previous correspondence, do so unobtrusively.

(Poor)   We have received your letter of April 15 in which you state that the order for 12 books which you placed by telephone on January 30 and which was to be shipped by Special 4th Class mail has not been received as of the date of writing.

(Better)   I have just checked with our shipping clerk and verified that your order for 12 books was shipped on February 15.

(Poor)   Replying to your October 16 communication, please accept our apologies for any inconvenience caused by the mistake we made in filling your last purchase order.

(Better)   Thank you for your October 16 letter pointing out our mistake in filling your last order.

A participle is a weak beginning for a letter. Avoid this kind of opening:

> Replying to your letter . . .
> Regarding our recent conversation . . .
> Knowing your interest in tennis . . .

Your reader wants to know quickly why you are writing; participial phrases seem like stalling tactics.

Have you tried beginning a sales letter with a question? I recently received a letter that started:

> What do tennis balls and our mailing list have in common?

I had to find out, so I read on. (The answer given was that the prices of both are the same as they were ten years ago.) Here are some other examples of opening questions:

> Are you certain your profit is real?
> How long has it been since you truly relaxed?
> Are you paying too much for life insurance?
> Do writing problems put your letters in the "Out" basket?

Look over some of your old letters; see if you can add interest by phrasing the first sentence as a question.

In some circumstances, a bold approach may win over the reader. When my son was looking for a summer job, he started his letter of application this way:

> I am writing to you because I need money to get to Philadelphia. Summer employment seems to offer the best way to earn that money.

The letter went on to list his qualifications and closed with the phone number where he could be reached to discuss employment — or to talk about why he wanted to go to Philadelphia. Not everyone will react favorably to such a daring approach. You must judge whether the risks outweigh the possible gains. In my son's case, the letter not only netted him a choice of summer jobs, but some recipients called just to tell him they liked the letter.

Whether you choose a bold or a conservative approach, step right into your subject to show the reader that you do not intend to waste valuable time. Make your first paragraph do something. For example, you might want to:

- express pleasure or regret;
- provide information;
- indicate an action taken;
- ask or answer a question.

Be sure your opening sets the right tone. Being direct and phrasing your words positively will help your reader form a favorable impression. Your first paragraph is both the headline and the lead for the message that follows:

> As soon as your letter arrived, we phoned your order to our St. Louis office.

> Your appointment as General Manager is good news indeed.

> You are right in assuming that we want to hear from our customers.

Avoid openings that restate the obvious:

> I have received your letter of October 16 . . .

have a negative tone:

> We cannot understand your failure to comply . . .

or contain cliches:

> At Fletcher's the customer is always right. So, better late than never . . .

See the sample letters presented in Chapter 4 for other ways to start your letters.

Brevity

Say what you have to say politely, clearly, and briefly. You show the greatest consideration for your reader when you take only enough time to convey what is important.

Art Seidenbaum, Book Editor for the *Los Angeles Times,* sent me what might be the ultimate in short letters. Art believes that every letter deserves an answer, be it ever so brief. I had requested that he include Periwinkle Press in his file of publisher's addresses, and his return letter consisted of one word, "Done."

I have made this letter longer than usual because I lack the time to make it shorter.—Pascal

---

Brevity is the natural result of using simple language. If you have used simple words and uncomplicated ways of expressing yourself, you have probably also been brief. It may take more time to write with fewer words, but doing so will prejudice the reader in your favor.

Closing Paragraphs

The chief function of your final paragraph is to bring your letter to a courteous, businesslike close. A summary of your main point is appropriate only if the letter is long. If action is called for, indicate what you want the reader to do or what you will do. Use positive words— "when" not "if."

(Poor)   Call me if you want more information.

(Better) I will gladly provide more detailed information—just give me a call.

(Poor)   I will try to call you next week to see if we can find a convenient time to get together.

(Better) I will call you next week to see when we can get together.

The amount of pressure you apply in your final paragraph depends on the nature of the letter. A goodwill letter that is primarily designed to keep in touch might end with a low-key "Let us hear from you when we can be of help." You apply a little more pressure if you ask a question: "May we send our sales representative, Marcia Wells, to demonstrate our new desktop model?" Strongly urging a specific action is the high-pressure end of the scale. The reader should understand why it is advantageous to comply, as in the following examples:

Use the enclosed information sheet to order your copies today. The books will be on their way to you promptly.

Just fill out and mail the enclosed questionnaire. By return mail we will send you a free 16-page booklet that's full of ways to stretch your food budget.

Please send your check to cover the overdue balance promptly. I'm sure you don't want such a small amount to jeopardize your credit rating.

A weak ending can diminish the effect of an otherwise well-written letter. Avoid the following:

Participial Phrases
>> Thanking you in advance
>> Hoping for a prompt reply

An Apologetic Attitude
>> I'm sorry I haven't been able to be of more help.

Cliches >> At this point in time
>> In the final analysis
>> Last but not least

Trivial Afterthoughts
>> By the way, the company soccer team
>> is doing quite well.

Make your closing sentences polite and to the point, and your reader will carry away a favorable impression.

Revising the Letter

When you have completed a letter, "change hats" from author to reader. Review what you have written as if you were seeing it for the first time. Ask yourself such questions as:

> Have I made my point?
> Do the sentences and ideas flow smoothly?
> Are the points of emphasis where I want them to be?
> Have I used the fewest possible words?

To answer these questions, you must put distance between you and your writing. If you can, put your letter aside for a while. A letter going to thousands of potential customers or to one potential employer is important enough to justify letting it "cool off" overnight. Having someone else go over the draft can also be helpful.

Revision is essential to the writing process—the best writers revise repeatedly. You will probably always want to revise long or particularly important letters. But shorter, more straightforward letters may need less revision as you develop your letter-writing talents. The editing process will begin to take place in your head, and you will find yourself able to choose the right words before you dictate or write them.

Form Letters,
Word Processor Style

A Word About Word Processors

Word processors offer the greatest potential for improving business letters since we stopped writing them by hand. How?

Word processors . . . Speed up production

Improve appearance

Facilitate revisions

Speed

You can easily catch and correct typographical errors on the word processor screen, *before* a letter is typed; furthermore, the machine does not introduce new typos when retyping, as humans are prone to do. Typing speed usually increases when the fear of making errors is eliminated.

Paragraphs or entire letters containing standard information can be stored, called from memory, modified if appropriate, and incorporated into a newly typed letter. The whole process takes just a fraction of the time required to produce a form letter with a standard typewriter.

Word processors also introduce new efficiencies in proofreading. A manually retyped letter must be checked carefully for new errors; only the changed portions of a letter typed on a word processor need to be proofed.

Appearance

Word processors help you produce attractive letters. Since typos are removed on the display screen, letters are blemish-free. There are no smudgy erasures or other telltale signs of correction to damage the professional image of your letter or detract from its message.

Letters always fit your letterhead. By entering standard formatting instructions, you can uniformly produce letters that are well-balanced and evenly spaced.

Revision

The most important contribution of word processors to better letters is the ability to revise at low cost. No longer should the expense of retyping make you hesitate to make changes. You can add or delete words, rearrange sentences, insert paragraphs, and print a new copy in minutes or even seconds. This gives you the freedom to revise until your words are just right—until the sales letter is the most persuasive, the proposal most convincing, the job application most effective.

Word Processors and Mass Mailings

Word processors offer additional capabilities that are often used in mass-mailed letters. By merging the text of a letter with a mailing list, you can address each letter to a specific individual. This distinguishes your letter from those beginning "Dear Homeowner"; it is well worth doing.

However, some other word processor capabilities are not as clearly a plus. For example, you can "personalize" your letter by repeating the recipient's name in the body of the letter. But would you do that when writing to someone you know? Probably not. This attempt to personalize letters backfires even more if a misspelling or error occurs when the name is entered. A typical result is the letter to the John Smith Family that begins "Dear Mr. & Mrs. Family"!

Word processors allow you to add visual interest or emphasis to your bulk-mailed letters. At the touch of a button you can underline or use boldface type. Unfortunately, this can make your letter look type*set* rather than type*written*.

Keep your letter from shouting "Junk Mail" by making it resemble an individually written letter as much as possible. Avoid using boldface type or inserting the recipient's name in the middle of a letter, even though it is easy to do so. Instead, put your word processor through its paces by polishing and perfecting your letter until it sparkles with originality—and "spontaneity."

In other words,

       revise . . .

              revise . . .

                    revise.

3
Business Letter Format

CHAPTER 3
Business Letter Format

First impressions count. They can determine whether your letter is read or simply thrown out. The first impression a letter makes is visual: Is the letter neat? Is it well placed on the page? Does it please the eye? Has a conventional format been used? These aspects of a letter can influence the reader as much as your choice of words.

Of course, no amount of visual appeal can make up for a poorly written letter. Ultimately, it has to stand on the strength of its content. But why cripple a well-written letter by putting it in an inferior package? By observing a few simple principles you can create a pleasing format that allows the reader to concentrate on the substance of your letter.

Format Styles

Format styles are identified as Full Block, Block, Semiblock, Modified Semiblock, and so on. Each secretarial handbook seems to have its own definition of these styles. The chief difference among them is placement of the date, complimentary close, and signature block. The easiest style to type is Full Block, because all lines begin flush with the left margin. However, some people prefer the more balanced appearance of letters in which the date and complimentary close begin near the middle of the page.

The main parts of a business letter are the date, inside address, salutation, body or text of the letter, complimentary close, signature, and typed name. All the format styles contain these basic elements. They may, in addition, have one or more of the optional lines frequently used in business letters, such as attention, reference, subject or identification lines; enclosure, distribution, mailing or carbon copy notations; or postscripts.

On the next page, the eight basic parts of a business letter are identified, and on the pages following are illustrations of the most commonly used letter format styles showing the correct placement of the letter parts, and of typical optional lines. Each of the styles is acceptable; the choice is one of personal preference — or company policy.

The F. L. Smith Co., Inc.
aajshd jasdfajkl
ajab jfhajskdjf ajskdlfsjakshd ajajhdfj
(123) ahsjdfajklas

Letterhead

May 17, 1993

Date

Inside Address

asdfhajsk lkasdfhaji
jyhcjakalskdj hjkdslasdf
asjdhfjqkejt djakals
jshdjfkalsdfhjl

Salutation

Dear ais Sashtljaksla.

Fhajsh jujch duai odfijudyfu isodt aa jty jonosi
a sudfyu asid fycovy oino aysdf susdfas adja asd ajsdhf
a abd ajdfyduyasdf aasdf asd a asdafyuqi3nof ahsjdfkl
ahsje jajsdfhajsk flkjhasafl.

Whajshajs fhajsdk lkasdfh kaghave a qkwerj.qwjerhj
ajsd.hajsk llfkdc jkasd jhajei ajsd qe ajdf jdex asdthiklas
snsjd asdfhe dcavdjjx dkajshdf ajas jahdf asdfhjklesaf ajsaf
kjsa aiskdfjkk.Lh ajdf a sdf ahsdjfi ajsk llasdfj.

Klala. fjahsdfha ajsdf asdfhq dfuc adjjasdf a sdfoai
a sdjdfsjd jsdjfk klasdjt ajs ajsjdhf skdlaje cuvlu dfaasdfi
njsdfha sja jd sksdfjd asdfuab dyausd ajdfhajklsd asd
asxa sjh a shd a sdfa

Body (Text) of Letter

Yours truly

Complimentary Close

Signature

John W. Kiakss

Typed Name

vs/s

Parts of the Letter

Optional Lines: attention, reference, subject, identification, enclosure, distribution, mailing notation, postscript.

Full Block

All lines begin flush with the left margin.
No indentations.
Dictator's initials are not included in the identification line.

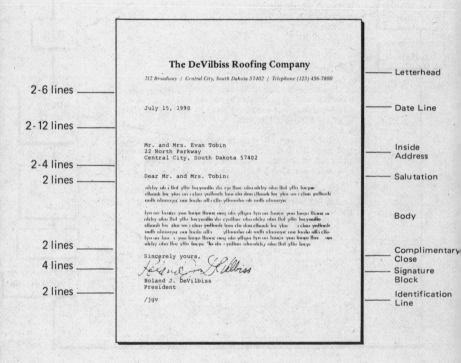

2-6 lines ——— Letterhead

The DeVilbiss Roofing Company

712 Broadway / Central City, South Dakota 57402 / Telephone (123) 456-7800

2-12 lines ——— Date Line

July 15, 1990

2-4 lines ——— Inside Address

Mr. and Mrs. Evan Tobin
22 North Parkway
Central City, South Dakota 57402

2 lines ——— Salutation

Dear Mr. and Mrs. Tobin:

Body

2 lines ——— Complimentary Close

Sincerely yours,

4 lines ——— Signature Block

Roland J. DeVilbiss
President

2 lines ——— Identification Line

/jgv

See p. 94 for an example of a Letter of Recommendation in Full Block style.

Block

Inside address and paragraphs are flush with the left margin.
Salutation and attention line are aligned with the inside address.
Date and reference lines are flush with the right margin.
Typed signature and complimentary close are aligned with the date.

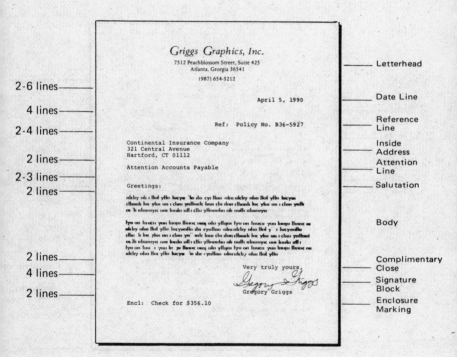

See p. 84 for an example of a Complaint Letter in Block style.

Semiblock

First line of each paragraph is indented five or ten spaces.
Date is flush with the right margin.
Complimentary close and typed signature are slightly to the right of center of the page.

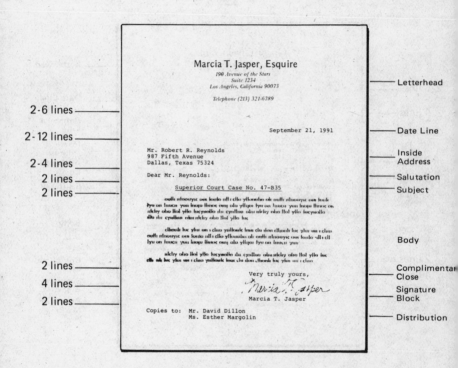

See p.*88* for an example of a Collection Letter in Semiblock style.

Official

Inside address is two to five lines below the signature; otherwise this style is the same as Semiblock.

Identification line and any enclosure notations are typed two lines below the address.

Used for personal letters in business.

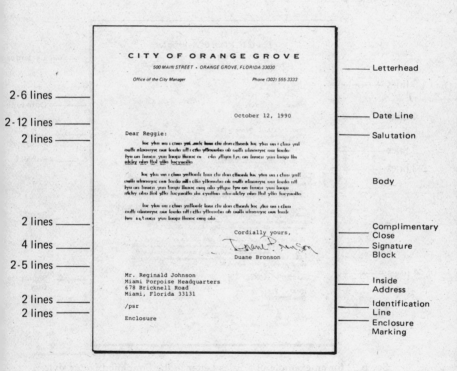

See p. 106 for an example of a Thank-You Letter in the Official style.

Simplified

No salutation or complimentary close.

All lines begin flush with the left margin.

Date is six lines below the letterhead.

Inside address is at least four lines below the date line.

Subject is typed in caps, three lines below the inside address and above the body of the letter.

Writer's name and title are typed in caps (on one or two lines), four or five lines below the body of the letter.

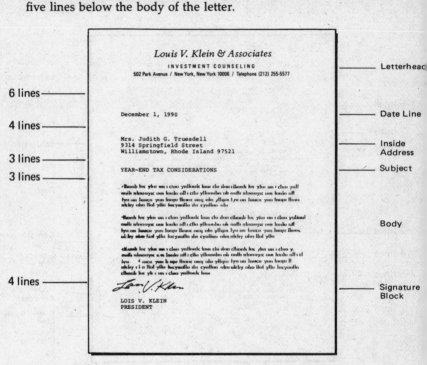

See p. 92 for an example of a Sales Letter in the Simplified Letter style.

The Simplified Letter may become increasingly popular. It provides the ultimate solution to the problem of a nonsexist salutation by eliminating it. When there is no salutation, you don't have to worry about the outmoded flavor of *Dear Sirs* or the gaffe of addressing a woman as *Mr.*

Memorandum

The memorandum format is used primarily for internal company communication; many companies have forms printed for this purpose. The following example illustrates a memo typed on plain paper.

```
TO:        Personnel Staff

FROM:      Irving Stern, Manager

DATE:      September 15, 1990

SUBJECT:   Screening Procedures


Effective immediately, all applicants for positions
with Hydrodynamics are to be given Personality
Adjustment Series J Tests.  These will replace the
Series H Test that was used previously.

The new series is both easier to administer and
to evaluate.  I trust you will find it helps your
task of selecting qualified candidates for
employment.
```

All lines start flush with the left margin. The heading begins about two inches from the top of the page. Double space between items in the heading, and align them as shown above, or as follows:

```
     TO:  Personnel Staff

   FROM:  Irving Stern, Manager

   DATE:  September 15, 1990

SUBJECT:  Screening Procedures


Effective immediately, all applicants for positions
with Hydrodynamics are to be given Personali
Adjustment Series J Tests.  These wil
```

Leave two or three blank lines between the heading and the text, which is usually single spaced. No signature is necessary since the name appears in the heading; however, the writer of the memo may place initials by his or her name or at the end of the text, if desired.

Placement on the Page

Center the text on the page. We've probably all received letters that fail to observe this simple rule — the short letter placed high on the page that looks as if the writer ran out of things to say too soon; or its opposite, the letter that is so crowded that the writer's signature barely fits on the page. Proper placement is simple if you follow a few rules.

Vary the margins according to the length of the letter.

> *Short letter* (body less than 100 words), about 4 inches wide; set margins at 35 and 75.

> *Average letter* (body 100-200 words), about 5 inches wide; set margins at 30 and 80.

> *Long letter* (body 200+ words), about 6 inches wide; set margins at 25 and 85.

In order to assist in setting margins, you can buy a letter placement guide similar to the one illustrated on the opposite page. Or you can make your own in the following way:

Place a heavy horizontal line at least a double space below the bottom line of the letterhead, to indicate the dateline; if a letterhead is not used, place the heavy line at least 12 single spaces from the top of the page. Add lines to indicate the margin for short, medium, and long letters. When you put the guide directly behind the original, you will be able to see the lines through the paper.

Set the margins directly over the appropriate line on the left and five spaces to the right of the corresponding line at the right-hand margin. Avoid letting more than a few letters of a word straggle over the right-hand margin. The numbers on the lower right-hand edge of the guide help determine the distance to the bottom of the page.

You can improve the overall appearance of a letter by varying the placement of certain lines.

To expand a letter to fill a page:

- Allow an additional blank line between text and complimentary close, or between close and signature;
- Type identifying initials and enclosure notations four to six lines below typed signature.

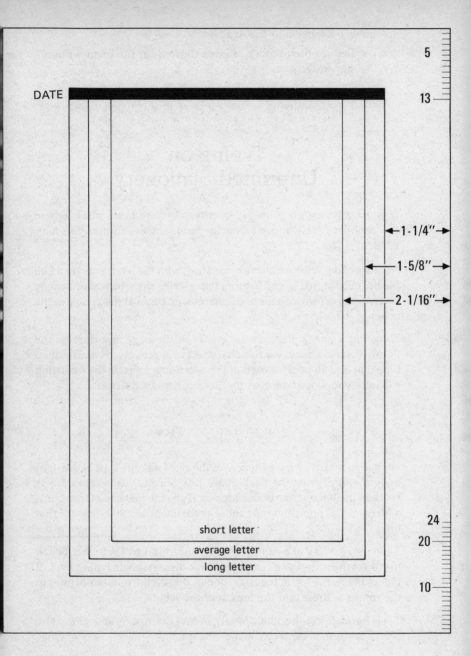

DATE

5

13

←1-1/4"→

←1-5/8"→

←2-1/16"→

short letter
average letter
long letter

24
20

10

51

To squeeze a letter into less space:

- Reduce the number of lines allowed for the hand-written signature;
- Eliminate company name in signature block;
- Type identifying initials on same line as typed signature.

Typing on
Unprinted Stationery

If you are typing on plain paper instead of letterhead, placement of the return address and dateline depends on the format you have chosen.

All lines of the return address begin flush with the left margin in a Full Block or Simplified Letter; in other letter styles, the return address may be centered, flush with the right margin, or begin at the center of the page.

To center a line, start from the center of the page and depress the Return Key once for every two characters or spaces of a given line, then type that line. Repeat for each of the remaining lines. In the following example you would depress the Return Key six times.

```
         1  2  3  4  5  6
```

FORMAT STYLES ◄ Don't count the
                  odd character

To place a return address flush with the right margin, start at the right margin and depress the Back Space Key once for each character or space in the longest line of the address. Type the *first* line of the return address at this point and type subsequent lines directly below the first line.

Type the first line of a centered return address 1 to 1½ inches below the top of the page. For all other return addresses, begin typing 1½ to 2 inches below the top of the page, depending on the number of lines in the return address and the length of the letter.

Type the date on the line directly below the return address; if the return address is centered, center the date as well.

Punctuating Parts
of the Letter

Style books describe letter punctuation as *open, closed,* and *mixed.* The rules vary even within those categories, however. One author's *open* is another's *mixed.* The following rules, frequently referred to as *mixed punctuation,* are traditional and easy to observe.

- No punctuation following the date or writer's name.

```
January 14, 1990
Miss Eve Adams
```

- No punctuation at the ends of address lines, other than a period following an abbreviation.

```
425 West Broadway
11500 Century Plaza, 11th Floor
```

- Colon following salutation in business letters; comma following salutation in social letters.

```
Dear Ms. Scott:
Dear Hank,
```

- Comma following complimentary close.

```
Yours truly,
```

Discussion of
Parts of the Letter

Date

Depending on the length of the letter, place the date on a single line
that is two to six lines below the printed address; three lines is standard
for most letters. Depending on letter style, place the date flush with the
right or left margin; you may also center the date if that blends well
with the letterhead.

Use the date on which the letter is dictated, even if it is typed at a later
date. Do not abbreviate or use figures for the month (for example, do
not type *Dec. 25* or *3/30/85*). Do not spell out or use *nd, th,* or *st* for the
day of the month, as in *September ninth* or *September 9th.* The order of
month and day may be reversed and the comma omitted when writing
to the U.S. Government, military personnel, or to correspondents in
foreign countries: 15 April 1990.

Inside Address

In all but the Official Style, place the inside address 2 to 12 lines below
the date, depending on the length of the letter. The inside address is
always flush with the left margin and should be single spaced. Any line
of the address that would extend much beyond the middle of the page
should be broken into two lines at a convenient spot, indenting the
carryover line two spaces:

> Ms. Gloria H. Templeton
> Tri-State Nickel Plate Quality Assurance
>   and Underwriters Association
> 1234 Business Street
> Everytown, New York 10022

When addressing a specific individual at a company, place the
individual's name on the first line, the company on the second. Use the
official company name, including abbreviations, capitalization,
ampersands (&), and other stylistic conventions employed by the
company you are addressing.

> The 3M Company, *not* Minnesota Mining & Manufacturing Co.

> Merrill Lynch, Pierce, Fenner & Smith, Inc., *not* Merrill, Lynch . . .

Place a person's title on the line with her or his name if the title is short; otherwise, place the title (no abbreviations) on the second line.

> Ms. Diane R. Webster, President

> Mr. Samuel V. Adams
> Vice President & General Manager

Business titles are frequently omitted because they make the address too long.

When addressing more than one individual, place the names on separate lines in alphabetical order.

> Ms. Joyce Ryder
> Mr. Sam Weingart

> Dear Ms. Ryder and Mr. Weingart:

> Mr. Alan English
> Ms. Ellen French

> Dear Mr. English and Ms. French:

> Mr. Daniel Longstreet
> Mr. Edwin Middleton

> Dear Messrs. Longstreet and Middleton:

Traditionally, if the gender of an individual is unknown, masculine titles are used. As one who frequently receives letters addressed to *Mr.* Jan Venolia and resents it, I approve of this modern-day alternative: Use the single capital letter *M*. This serves as an abbreviation of an abbreviation and provides a convenient solution to the unknown gender problem.

When the letter is addressed to a specific department within a company rather than to an individual, type the company name on the first line and the department on the second.

> Sears, Roebuck & Co.
> Credit Department
> 1234 Sears Tower
> Chicago, Illinois 60611

Place suite, room, or apartment numbers *after* and on the same line as the street address, separated by a comma.

> 1234 Spring Street, Suite 1157
> Los Angeles, California 90017

If both street address and post office box appear on the company stationery, use the post office box. Place any postal station after the post office box.

> P.O. Box 1357, Terminal Annex   *or* P.O. Box 1357
> Terminal Annex

When you list both a street address and a post office box, the post office will send your letter to whichever is directly above the bottom line.

> Acme Printers   Acme Printers
> 20247 Broad Street   P.O. Box 1305
> • P.O. Box 1305   • 20247 Broad Street
> New Town, CA 91365   New Town, CA 91367

Mail directed to the street address of a company that has a post office box will go through a forwarding process that may take one day longer to arrive. Thus, the left-hand address above will provide speedier delivery. The best way to avoid confusion is to omit the street when you are addressing mail to a post office box.

Since the post office prefers that two-letter state abbreviations be used for outside addresses, some secretarial schools teach students to use these abbreviations for inside addresses as well. Restrictions imposed by word processors on the number of characters in the address block may also force you to abbreviate. However, your letter will have a more professional appearance if you spell out all words of inside addresses whenever possible.

Spell out compass directions that *precede* the street name; abbreviate those *following* it.

> 1234 West Orange Street
> 567 Lemon Street S.W.

The word *one* is written out in a street address:

> One Market Street

Numbered streets are written as words for ten and below, as figures above ten.

        300 Seventh Avenue
        750 - 12th Street

When compass directions *precede* a numbered street, use cardinal numbers (1, 2, 3 ...); otherwise, use ordinal numbers (1st, 2nd, 3rd ...) and insert a hyphen between building or house number and street number; put a space on each side of the hyphen.

        8147 East 42 Street
        640 - 65th Avenue

Salutations

The standard *Dear Mrs. Phillips* or *Dear John* is appropriate for most situations, including the very formal. *My dear Mrs. Phillips* is out of step with today's business world, and salutations such as that are now used only when addressing dignitaries.

The salutation is followed by a colon in business letters and by a comma in social letters (especially handwritten ones). The salutation is typed flush with the left margin, two to four lines below the inside address or the attention line (if one is used).

Titles

It is customary to precede an individual's name with a courtesy title such as *Mr., Mrs., Miss, Ms., Dr.,* or *Professor.* In the United States, if an abbreviation or a degree (for example, *Ph.D.*) or the word *Esquire* follows the name, omit the courtesy title. *Esquire* (or *Esq.*) may be used when addressing professional persons such as attorneys or consuls.

Wrong:	Right:
Dr. Manley Beacon, Ph.D.	Manley Beacon, Ph.D.
Dr. Adrian Condon, M.D.	Adrian Condon, M.D.
Ms. Carol Thomas, Esq.	Carol Thomas, Esq.
Honorable Roy McNeill, Esq.	Honorable Roy McNeill
Mr. Jose M. Juarez, Esquire	Jose M. Juarez, Esquire

In the United Kingdom, *Esq.* is used when addressing people who have distinguished themselves professionally or diplomatically; it may appear with another title.

> Howard R. Heath, Esq., LL.D.
>
> Arthur J. Shaw, Esq., M.D.

Although *Esquire* has a masculine flavor, you may use it for both sexes.

Use of a comma before the title *Jr.* or *Sr.* is optional. Follow the preference of the individual, if you know it.

> Edwin R. Turner, Jr.   *or*   Edwin R. Turner Jr.

Be sure to put a comma between *Jr.* or *Sr.* and an abbreviation or professional rating:

> Duane C. Holtzman, Jr., M.D.
>
> Malcolm V. Vincent Jr., Esq.

The designation *Sr.* is not used unless identical names are closely associated, as in a family business. *Jr.* and *Sr.* are usually dropped after the death of the father or son.

Multiple Addressees

Messrs. (abbreviation of the word *Messieurs,* which is the plural form of *Mr.)* may be used when addressing more than one male. Address more than one female as *Mesdames, Mmes.,* or *Mses.* Omit first names when using these abbreviations.

> Wrong: Messrs. John Johnson, Ian Jones, and Tim Smith
> Right: Messrs. Johnson, Jones and Smith
>
> Wrong: Mses. Marion Gordon and Juanita Hernandez
> Right: Mses. Gordon and Hernandez

Women

A host of problems confront the person addressing a woman. Should you use *Mrs.* or *Ms.,* a married woman's first name or her husband's? And what about divorcees or widows? The best guide is what the woman herself prefers, if that is known. If you have a signed letter, use the form she has chosen. Lacking that information, use the following guidelines.

- Use *Ms.* if marital status is unknown.

- In business, use a married woman's first name (Mrs. Evelyn Stone); socially, the custom has been to use her husband's first name (Mrs. Stephen Stone). However, customs change, and the choice of names is now more a matter of personal preference than it was in the past. See Chapter 6, *Dear Sir or Madam.*

- For a widowed or divorced woman, use her first name and married name, unless she has chosen to return to her maiden name. In general, use *Mrs.* when addressing married, widowed, or divorced women, unless you know that *Ms.* is preferred.

Couples

You have additional choices when addressing a couple where one or both are titled. When the husband has a title, the customary address is Dr. and Mrs. William Karl or Judge and Mrs. Vincent Green. When both have a title or only the woman has a title, the possibilities are numerous. The traditional approach would be to drop the woman's title: Mr. and Mrs. Sylvan Campbell. But these are not traditional days, and the following alternatives will probably be used more and more frequently.

When both have a title:

> Drs. Susan and Sean McIntyre
> Dr. Susan McIntyre and Dr. Sean McIntyre
> Drs. Sean and Susan McIntyre

When only the woman has a title:

> Dr. Karen Johnson and Mr. Philip Johnson
> Dr. Karen and Mr. Philip Johnson

Whenever it is known, use the form preferred by the individual(s) you are addressing. A person is usually sensitive about his or her name and will notice if you get it right—or wrong.

Unknown Addressee

The salutation *To Whom It May Concern* is no longer appropriate. Use the Simplified Letter form (see p. *48*) for a letter of recommendation or a character reference when you don't know the name of the addressee.

A letter addressed to a company but not to a specific individual presents the problem of finding a neutral salutation without making an awkward substitution. *Dear Sir or Madam* is a good example of an awkward substitution. Many alternatives have been suggested:

Dear Friend	Dear Colleague
Dear Customer	Dear Reader

Each has its drawbacks. *Dear Friend* may sound presumptuous, *Dear Customer* too cold, *Dear Colleague* inaccurate, and *Dear Reader* may suggest that the letter has been retrieved from a bottle.

Another suggestion is to replace the words *Dear Sir* or *Gentlemen* with *Greetings.* Or you might use the memo format, an example of which appears on p. *49* . If the memo appears too informal, perhaps the Simplified Letter provides a better solution. For a more complete discussion of this and other aspects of sexist terms in letters, see Chapter 6, *Dear Sir or Madam.*

Typing the Body of the Letter

Begin the message three lines below the subject line in Simplified Letters and two lines below the salutation or subject line in all other letter styles. Use single space for most letters. If the letter is very short, use space-and-a-half or double space. Indent paragraphs five or ten spaces when using Semiblock or Official styles, or when the letter is double-spaced. Double space between paragraphs.

Numbered material in the body of the letter is indented five spaces or centered. The number is followed by a period or is enclosed in parentheses; allow one or two spaces after the period or closing parenthesis. Punctuation either follows each numbered item or none of them. Double space between items.

> (1) Physical Fitness
>
> (2) Effects of Stress
>
> (3) Nutrition

Or, start the second and subsequent lines of each item directly below the first word of the item.

> 1. Sales Staff
>   a. Local
>   b. State
>   c. National
>
> 2. Advertising
>   a. Television and Radio Spots
>   b. Print Media
>
> 3. Objectives of the Program
>   by Individual Areas

Letters of More Than One Page

Printed letterhead should be used only for the first page of a letter. If the letter consists of more than one page, continuation pages should be typed on plain sheets that match the letterhead paper or on printed second sheets. (On printed second sheets, the company name appears in smaller type than that of the letterhead, and the company address is omitted.)

The heading should begin six lines below the top of the page and should contain the name of the recipient, page number, and date.

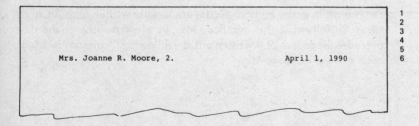

```
                                                                          1
                                                                          2
                                                                          3
                                                                          4
                                                                          5
   Mrs. Joanne R. Moore, 2.                      April 1, 1990            6
```

Leave four or five lines between the heading and the body of the letter. At least two lines of text should be on the page with the complimentary close.

When you write to more than one individual at a firm:

```
                                                              1
                                                              2
                                                              3
                                                              4
                                                              5
     Mr. Henry Burr                                           6
     Mr. James Thompson                                       7
     American Book Company            May 14, 1990
```

If Full Block style is used:

```
                                                              1
                                                              2
                                                              3
                                                              4
                                                              5
     Johnson Brothers, Inc.                                   6
     Page 2                                                   7
     May 22, 1990                                             8
```

Dates written in the body of a letter are usually written without an *st, nd,* or *th* following the number (May 9, *not* May 9th). If the day precedes the month or is written out, the following forms may be used: *ninth of May,* or *9th of May.*

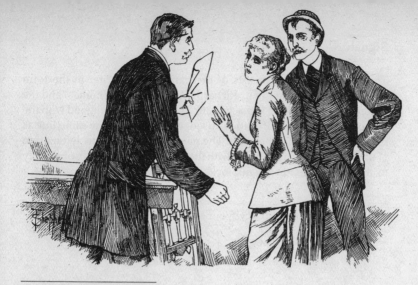

Complimentary Close

The complimentary close is placed two lines below the body of the letter, either flush with the left margin (Full Block), aligned with the date (Block), or slightly to the right of center (Semiblock, Official). It should never extend beyond the right margin established by the body of the letter.

Capitalize only the first letter of the first word of a complimentary close. The closing is followed by a comma.

Highly Formal (diplomatic or ecclesiastic correspondence)	Respectfully yours, Respectfully,
Polite, Formal (general correspondence)	Very truly yours, Yours truly,
Less Formal	Sincerely yours, Sincerely, Cordially,
Informal, Friendly	As ever, Best regards, Kindest regards,

Signature

The signature block consists of the name of the writer in the form preferred by the writer (e.g., Richard P. Thomas, R.P. Thomas) and the writer's title. The name is placed four lines below and aligned with the complimentary close. If a title is used, it is placed on the same line as the name, or one line below it. The name is flush with the left margin (Full Block, Simplified), flush with the right margin (Block), or slightly to the right of center (Semiblock, Official).

Very truly yours,

Richard P. Thomas

Richard P. Thomas, President

Sincerely yours,

R. P. Thomas

R. P. Thomas
Vice President and General Manager

In the Simplified Letter, the writer's name is typed all in caps, flush with the left margin, four or five lines below the body of the letter.

In formal letters requiring the company name as part of the signature (especially in letters of a contractual nature), the company name is typed in capital letters two spaces below the complimentary close, and the writer's name four spaces below the company name.

Very truly yours,

MORRISON MANUFACTURING COMPANY

Deborah Morrison

Deborah Morrison, President

If the letter deals with personal matters, omit the writer's title. The writer's typed name may be omitted if it appears in the letterhead.

When a letter states a professional opinion or gives professional advice, some lawyers and accountants prefer to sign the company name rather than the individual writer's name. In this case, the word *By* and a line for the signature of the writer are usually placed four spaces below the company name.

                    Very truly yours,

                    Holmes, Wasserman, and Dennis
                    A Legal Corporation

                    By *Malcolm V. Dennis*

                       Malcolm V. Dennis, Partner

Mrs., Miss, and *Ms.* are the only titles that precede the writer's typed name, and their use is optional. When used, they are enclosed in parentheses.

        (Mrs.) Carol Friedman

                    (Miss) Doris Radcliff

In social letters, a married woman customarily types her husband's name, preceded by *Mrs.,* and encloses the entire name in parentheses.

                Sincerely yours,

                Ethyl Davis
                (Mrs. Peter S. Davis)

A widow may continue to sign her name as she did before her husband's death.

A divorced woman's typed signature should be the same as the handwritten one and should use her first name and her former husband's surname, unless she has chosen to return to her maiden name. The title *Mrs.* in parentheses preceding her name is optional.

Right: Wrong:

Yvonne Young   *Yvonne Young*
(Mrs.) Yvonne Young   (Mrs. John T. Young)

If you are signing a letter for the person who dictated it, place your initials just below and to the right of the signature.

Sincerely yours,

Richard P. Thomas

Richard P. Thomas, President   Z.J.

When you write a letter on behalf of your employer or supervisor (that is, when you actually compose the letter, not just type it), sign your own name directly above the typed title: Secretary to Mr. Thomas. Omit the employer's first name and initial unless they are needed for identification.

Very truly yours,

Ellen Bowen

Secretary to Mr. Thomas

Optional Features

An *attention line* indicates that a letter is strictly business and assures that it will be opened in the absence of the individual whose name appears in the line. The attention line is placed two spaces below the bottom line of the inside address, flush with the left margin (Full Block,

Block, Simplified Letter) or centered. The word *of* is not necessary, and a colon following the word *Attention* is optional. Do not underline or use all capital letters.

Attention lines are more impersonal than a direct address and should be used only when appropriate. They are helpful if you don't know a person's first name.

Acceptable: Preferred:

Attention Mr. Vincent   Attention Mr. Samuel R. Vincent

See p. 74 for placement of the attention line on the outside address.

In the past, the correct salutation following an address with an attention line was *Gentlemen*. To many individuals in business today, this salutation is as unacceptable as *Dear Sir*. Appropriate substitutes are discussed in Chapter 6, *Dear Sir or Madam*.

If an incoming letter has a *reference line,* type the number cited about four lines below the date line in your response. If your company also has a policy of using file references, place your own reference number one line below the incoming reference, unless your letterhead has a printed section for it. Reference lines are typical of government correspondence or can be helpful when writing about an order.

KARLA HATS CO

410 Cambridge Ave.
Buffalo, New York 14225

(716) 123-4567

October 22, 1990

Reference: P.O. #593-82E
Our File Ref.:   Invoice #6829

The *subject line* identifies the content of the letter in a few well-chosen words. It is part of the body of the letter and thus is centered below the salutation, about two spaces. In the Simplified Letter, which has no salutation, the subject line is placed three lines below the last line of the inside address.

The subject may be preceded by the word *Subject,* followed by a colon. Use all caps and no underlining, or capitalize the first letter in each important word and underline the entire subject line.

SUBJECT: THE ANNUAL SHAREHOLDERS' MEETING

or

New Accounting Procedures

A subject line is a convenience to the reader and to the filing clerk. However, it imparts a "memorandum" flavor to the letter and is difficult to use when more than one subject is covered.

The *identification line* is for the convenience of the company issuing the letter; it should contain only the lowercase initials of the typist when the name of the person dictating the letter appears in the signature.

Sincerely yours,

Virginia Holt

Virginia Holt, Manager
Public Relations

pm

Many organizations place identifying initials only on copies of the letter, for recordkeeping purposes. The initials are usually typed flush with the left margin, two lines below the signature block.

Some companies prefer to show a complete identification line; in that case, type the dictator's initials in caps, flush left, two lines below the signature block; the typist's initials follow a colon or slash and are in lowercase.

Yours truly,

Daniel F. Painter

Daniel F. Painter

DFP/jg

If the person signing the letter did not dictate it, his or her initials are typed in capital letters, followed by those of the person dictating the letter (also in caps) and the typist (lowercase). The initials are separated by colons or slashes.

Yours truly,

Sylvia E. Langford

Sylvia E. Langford

SEL:DRM:pd

Sincerely,

Eric Hofstad

Eric Hofstad

EH/FVR/be

Enclosure markings serve both as a check to the recipient of the letter that everything was actually enclosed and as a reminder to the letter writer of what was sent. The word *enclosure(s)* or the abbreviation *Enc.* (or *Encl.*) is typed flush left, two spaces below the identification line (if one shows on the original). If more than one document is enclosed, list the number in parentheses. If the items are of importance, identify them, one per line. If any are to be returned, indicate this with a parenthetical notation following the item.

Very truly yours,

Joseph R. Danvers

Joseph R. Danvers

Enc.:   Check for $101.50
        Resale Tax Card

Very truly yours,   Sincerely yours,

Diane Peterson   *Peter D. Stuyvesant*

Diane Peterson   Peter D. Stuyvesant

DP/kr   kr

Enclosures (3)   2 Encs.

Very truly yours,

Janet F. Goldman

Janet F. Goldman

Encl.:   Draft Agreement (please return)

The skilled typist uses identification lines and enclosure markings to balance the letter on the page. If the letter is a little high, drop these notations two lines below the signature block; if the letter fills the page, place them on the same line as the typewritten signature.

If you wish the recipient to know of *distribution* of copies of the letter, type *Copy to* and the name of the individual(s) flush left, two lines below all other notations (if space allows). The abbreviation *cc* (carbon copy) followed by a colon may also be used.

```
            Very truly yours,

            MARK L. RIVERS

            Mark L. Rivers
            Treasurer

            Enclosures

            Copy to Mrs. Betty Goldwater
```

```
            cc:  Dr. Irene M. Mathis
                 745 California Street
                 Spokane, WA 98101
```

If you do not want the recipient to know of any copy distribution, a blind copy notation is entered *only* on copies of the letter, not the original. The abbreviation *bcc* (blind carbon copy) is placed in the upper left corner of the letter, followed by a colon and the names.

Mailing notations, such as Express Mail, Special Delivery, or any other unusual method, should be made on copies of the letter, but not the original.

If a business letter is personal, the word *Personal* or *Confidential* should be written and underlined at the top of the letter, about four lines above the address. Reserve the use of this notation for matters that are strictly personal, rather than as a device to catch someone's attention.

```
            Confidential

            Edward F. Lloyd, Esq.
            Citizens Bank Building
            Suite 1452
            100 Sycamore Street
            St. Louis, Missouri 67234
```

It is also important to type *Personal* or *Confidential* on the envelope, a double space above and just to the left of the address.

WILLIAM BROWN CO., INC.
   One Maritime Plaza
   Miami, Florida 32711

                              Confidential

                                 Edward F. Lloyd, Esq.
                                 Citizens Bank Building
                                 Suite 1452
                                 St. Louis, Missouri 67234

A *postscript* is typed flush left, two to four spaces below the last notation; you do not need to use the initials P.S. preceding the postscript. Use postscripts sparingly; they should never suggest that you omitted information and had to tack it on at the end. But since they do catch the reader's eye, postscripts can be used effectively in a sales letter.

Mark Twain put the postscript to good use in the following letter to Andrew Carnegie:

Dear Sir and Friend:

You seem to be in prosperity. Could you lend an admirer $1.50 to buy a hymn-book with? God will bless you. I feel it; I know it. So will I.

                              Yours,

                              Mark

P.S. Don't send the hymn-book; send the money; I want to make the selection myself.

                              M.

July 8, 1990

Leslie Williams
One Spring Street
St. Louis, Missouri 67830

Dear Subscriber:

Your subscription to listener-supported television will expire
soon. The support you have given us has helped maintain
the high standards of television programming you have come
to associate with WXYZ.

Let me give you a preview of some of our plans for the
upcoming season:

    -The highly acclaimed children's series, Poppyseed Place,
will present its twelfth year of educational fun.

    -Sports enthusiasts can choose from World Cup Soccer,
tennis instruction, and Olympic retrospectives.

    -Film buffs will enjoy our continuing series of cinema
classics, this year covering the decade from 1930 to 1940.

    -We are bringing back live television drama with the
revival of Playhouse 100. Some of our country's most talented
actors will take part in this 25-week series.

    -A 12-part documentary on successful social programs
will provide a refreshing counter-balance to the daily, and
often depressing, news.

In this brief letter, it's hard to suggest the broad scope of
programs available on WXYZ. But it's not hard to know who
makes them possible--you! With your continued support, we
will have an exciting year ahead.

Sincerely yours,

Lee R. Tompkins

Lee R. Tompkins

P.S. If you renew your subscription in the next two weeks,
     during our annual membership drive, we will send you
     a surprise gift. Our way of saying, "Thank you."

Envelopes

The post office states that you will receive the best service if your envelope addresses comply with the following guidelines:

- Use all capital letters.
- Eliminate punctuation.
- Abbreviate according to the list of common abbreviations in the ZIP Code Directory (AVE, ST, APT, S, W, RT, etc.).
- Use the two-letter state abbreviations.
- Put two spaces between the word groups (e.g., between street address and suite number) and two to five spaces between the state abbreviation and ZIP Code.
- Avoid italic or script type.

Include the following elements in both the sender's and the recipient's address:

- Name of the individual and/or company,
- Street address (with any apartment or suite number on the same line),
- City, state, and ZIP Code.

Single space the address, roughly centered on the lower half of the envelope. Type notations regarding special methods of mailing, such as Special Delivery or Express Mail, in caps below where the stamps will be placed.

Place an attention line on the second line, below the company name.

```
ECKHARDT EXPORTS INC
ATTN JONAS WILLIAMS
ONE SPRING STREET
MIAMI   FL   33033
```

```
Hamerslag Corporation
37 Keltenstrasse
CH 4106   Basel
Switzerland
```

```
HAMERSLAG CORP
37 KELTENSTR
CH 4106  BASEL
SWITZERLAND
```

Foreign countries are typed all in caps on the envelope, but with initial caps only on inside addresses.

4
Business Letters

CHAPTER 4

Business Letters

Words mean business—literally. Your written words influence the reader's opinion about doing business with you or your company. When your letter is read, you will not be present to correct wrong impressions or add missing information; for the moment, the words you put on the page have to do the whole job of representing you.

The first thing the recipient notices is the appearance of the letter. Just as you wouldn't want an unkempt salesman with gravy on his tie representing you, you don't want a poorly spaced letter with smudgy corrections to be the vehicle for your words. The business letter that conveys a professional image will be neat, have few (if any) corrections, and will be well placed on the page. (See Chapter 3.)

All letters should be regarded as sales letters, though their immediate function may be as a cover letter or a request for information. But not all letters have to engage the reader's interest as sales letters do. Streamline your letters to suit their purpose, eliminating jargon or unnecessary words without sacrificing clarity, completeness, or courtesy. (See Chapter 1.)

The letters that follow are typical of business correspondence; they are meant to suggest, not to prescribe. Use them to spark your own ideas about letters for your particular client, prospective employer, or delinquent account.

The Cover Letter
(Transmittal Letter)

Cover letters may be one or two sentences describing what is enclosed or a full page that adds a selling message to the accompanying document.

> Our check for $38.00 is attached. Please enter a one-year subscription to *Business World* and send it to the address appearing in our letterhead.
>
> Thank you.

•

As promised, I enclose a copy of the article on NOW checking accounts that we discussed. It should answer all of your questions, but if you need additional information, just give me a call.

●

The cost of heating or cooling a home is no longer an insignificant part of the household budget. Inflation and higher energy costs have forced homeowners to choose heating and cooling equipment with care.

The enclosed booklet describes solar-powered as well as conventional equipment that is available today. The brochure examines types of equipment and compares energy efficiencies of various models.

This booklet is part of an ongoing commitment to keeping our customers informed on energy-related matters. We welcome your comments or questions.

●

The enclosed proposal outlines our plan to improve employee productivity in your Parks and Recreation Department. Our program enables you to stretch both financial and human resources without laying off employees or reducing responsiveness to the public.

Mr. Thomas Darby will head our staff of specialists, who bring to this assignment a combined total of 50 years of experience in related fields. Mr. Darby will report their findings to you each month.

In similar programs, we have increased productivity by 33 to 75 percent. We developed better communication between staff and management, and between department personnel and the public. The mechanisms we installed for airing grievances markedly improved employee morale.

I believe you will find our program to be a powerful ally in tackling the problems of a restricted budget and inflationary pressures.

●

Letters of Inquiry

Perhaps the chief point to remember about letters of inquiry is that you must provide sufficient detail to obtain the desired action or information. If you are responding to an advertisement or other promotional medium, mention the name or source of your information. Be sure your address is in the letterhead or body of the letter.

Your ad in the June issue of *Management News* indicates that you sell business forms. Does that include forms to be used with computerized equipment? If so, please send information on prices and availability of the following items:

1. tractor-fed mailing labels, pressure-sensitive, two-across
2. invoices (carbonless and with carbons), four-part
3. tractor-fed ledgers (A/R, A/P, general ledger)

Thank you for your help.

●

Your ideas about the psychological effects of color and lighting are thought-provoking. I read about your research in the November issue of *Corporate Office,* and since we plan to redecorate our offices soon, we would like to learn more about your findings.

I would appreciate receiving a copy of the booklet that was mentioned in the article. Please send it to my attention at the above address. Thank you.

●

Will you please send me a copy of your current catalog and price list? We are planning to purchase a desktop photocopier for our staff of six and estimate monthly use at 500-1,000 copies.

Eventually we will want a demonstration of your equipment in our office, but now we are chiefly interested in receiving descriptive literature. We appreciate your help.

●

Unsolicited Request

Some inquiries are unsolicited; that is, they are not in response to an advertisement, listing in the Yellow Pages, or other promotional medium. These letters ask a favor of the recipient, since they take time to answer and may require some research. You will achieve the highest rate of response if your letters include the following:

1) a clear statement of the kind of information you are seeking;
2) a minimum number of questions, phrased to be easy to answer;
3) an explanation of why your reader would want to respond;
4) an expression of appreciation;
5) a self-addressed stamped envelope (if possible).

•

Some of our subscribers don't hesitate to tell us what they think of us. If an article offends or angers or pleases them, we hear about it. But for every reader of *News & Views* who writes to us, thousands remain silent.

I would like to change that situation. We want to know what you like and don't like about our magazine . . . what interests you, which stories you want us to cover, and which items you prefer that we leave to our competitors.

To show our appreciation for your filling out our questionnaire, I enclose a pocket almanac. You will find it packs a great deal of useful information into a small amount of space—not unlike *News & Views*.

Request for Action

Our computer recently flagged your account because it is missing some information required by the Internal Revenue Service. Will you please enter your social security number on the enclosed card and mail it to us today? Thank you for your cooperation.

•

In order to qualify for tax-free sales, you must provide certain information about your store. Please fill out and return the enclosed resale tax card when you send us your check for Invoice No. 1492.

Response to Inquiries

When you respond to inquiries, whether spontaneous or solicited by some form of advertising, you write from a privileged position. Your readers have already shown an interest in what you will write. If you fail to capitalize on this interest, you pass up an excellent opportunity to promote your products and to establish good customer relations (i.e., good will).

To build on existing interest:

- respond promptly;
- spell names and addresses correctly;
- set a friendly, positive tone without applying pressure;
- provide all the information requested; if unable to do so, explain why;
- make subsequent action by the potential customer easy.

Imagine yourself as the customer who knows nothing about the product or service. What information would you need in order to make the decision to buy? Emphasize those aspects you believe are of most interest to the individual you are addressing. Anticipate questions or problems and answer them up front.

You may accomplish all these objectives by a well-written form letter. But be sure it doesn't *seem* like a form letter. Changing a few words or a paragraph may be all that's needed to personalize your response to each inquiry.

> The information you requested is contained in the enclosed booklet, "Home Insulation: Costs and Benefits." We are pleased to have this chance to spread the good news about how insulating your home can cut heating bills. A bonus you may not be aware of is how much more comfortable you and your family will be when your house is insulated with Jiffy Foam.
>
> If you would like an estimate of the cost of insulating your home, we would be happy to drop by for a consultation. Indicate the most convenient time on the enclosed postcard, or give us a call at 666-1300. As a service to working families, our estimators make appointments for weekday evenings and on Saturday from 9 to 5.
>
> Thank you for your interest.

Thank you for your letter of July 15 inquiring about NBS franchises in the Western States. We do have opportunities available in two areas: Seattle and Phoenix. Those locations offer a distinct choice of climate, but each has the same solid prospect for a healthy return on your investment.

I enclosed a prospectus that describes the NBS franchise in detail. The variety of support services we provide for our franchise holders is a source of pride to us here at NBS headquarters. I will be glad to send you the names and phone numbers of several franchisees in your area if you want to hear firsthand about the benefits of being in the NBS family.

I hope this information will help you decide to join us. If I can be of any help, please give me a call.

Claim Letters
(Letters of Complaint)

When you are writing a claim letter, you may be frustrated or angry, or both. But the person who reads your letter will seldom be the one who created the problem; instead, that person is the one you want to help you straighten it out. Thus, you should avoid threats, sarcasm, and accusations. If you have a legitimate complaint, just presenting the facts will reveal it.

A claim letter should include the following elements:

Statement of claim

> "One of the correcting typewriter ribbons in my last order was defective."

Details needed for identification (include dates, model numbers, color, size, etc., where appropriate)

> "I enclose a copy of the invoice that shows the type of ribbon and date of purchase."

Proposed corrective action

> "Your customer service rep stated that you would arrange to have UPX pick up the defective ribbon; I understand that I have a choice between a credit to my account for the full purchase price or a replacement ribbon. I prefer that you send a replacement as soon as possible, since I anticipate a heavy typing load in the next few weeks.

Positive closing, expressing confidence that your request will be met

> "I appreciate your help in this matter. I have come to rely on the quality of IBX products and on your service to customers."

```
                                   1369 Dartmouth Lane, Apt. 61
                                   Evanston, Illinois 60493
                                   September 11, 1990


Brandhoff's Department Store
Accounts Payable
Center Shopping Mall
Evanston, Illinois 60490

Dear Computer:

I have never written a letter to a computer before, but it
seemed the only appropriate action left to me.  You and I
are locked in an unending dance, the steps of which are
roughly as follows:

   (1) You write a letter stating that charges to my account
       at Brandhoff's have exceeded the allowed limit.  You
       request payment for the excess as well as the monthly
       balance due.

   (2) I respond (letter dated 7/15/90) reporting that my
       April payment of $152.83 was never credited to my
       account, hence the problem.  I offer to send a copy
       of the cancelled check.

   (3) Repeat of Step (1).  Letter slightly more urgent.

   (4) I respond (letter dated 9/21/90) by sending a copy of
       both sides of my cancelled check for payment of the
       April charges, which still have not been credited to
       my account.

   (5) Repeat of Step (1).  Letter borders on threatening.

Having failed to correct the situation with Steps 2 & 4,
I am appealing to you directly (Step 6).  It seems clear
that I have taken all the necessary actions to confirm
timely payment.  I hope my appeal convinces you or your
operator to remove my name from your list of Bad Guys
and restore it to your list of Good Guys.

                           Sincerely,

                           Christopher Kelly

                           Christopher Kelly
```

Sample Complaint Letter written in Block format.

Author's Note: I have addressed several letters to computers when conventional efforts
have failed. It has worked every time.

Collection Letters

Collection letters are sent to customers who haven't paid their bills. Such letters are referred to as the "collection series," because more than one letter is often needed to accomplish the objective. The letters move from gentle reminders to heavy artillery. Yet each letter in the series must be written as if you expect it to be the last—as if this is the one that will do the trick.

Collection letters perform more than one function. In addition to their primary purpose of collecting overdue accounts, they are an important sales tool. In fact, the effective collection letter has much in common with the sales letter; it sells the customer the idea of paying the bill.

In most cases, you want to retain the overdue account as a customer. But even if you would prefer never to do business with a customer again, you stand the best chance of collecting the amount due if you avoid words that irritate or antagonize. A genuinely disgruntled customer can lead to the loss of more than one account.

Collection letters should reveal an understanding of the customer's position (the "you" attitude); the accusatory tone of "me vs. you" is unproductive. At first, assume the customer wants to pay and just needs a little reminding. But even your early reminders should not have the appearance or flavor of a form letter; they should read and look as if they were directed right at the reader. Customers who sense that you have sent a form letter may be encouraged to delay payment a little longer. You send signals of not yet taking a real interest in the case if your letter suggests it is "Letter B-2: Delinquent Accounts, 30-60 Days."

Timing is important. The interval between letters should allow for a response and for the possibility that the recipient is ill or out of town. The customer's credit rating will also influence timing: those with an excellent rating should be allowed a liberal amount of time between letters, while those with a record of slow payment or a poor credit rating would probably receive more frequent notices, with a stronger tone.

The first collection letter will probably be sent after the customer has received the original invoice and a follow-up statement; here you simply draw attention to the overdue amount in a friendly tone. In the letter that follows, you can inquire if there is a reason for the delay—something lost in the mail, an error in the records, or possibly dissatisfaction with the goods or service.

The next letter in the series assumes that the previous assumption was mistaken and that, in fact, the customer is deliberately delinquent. At this point you appeal to the customer's sense of responsibility and fair play as well as to self-interest (protecting credit rating). If you approach these letters with a light touch, using humor or even a gimmick to attract attention, your chance of success will be improved.

The final letter in the series assumes that the customer will pay only if forced to do so. The threats you employ depend on how you intend to pursue the matter. If you plan to turn the case over to a collection agency or an attorney, make it clear that the customer can still avert this drastic action. But do not make empty threats; advise the customer only of those actions you will actually take.

A series of collection letters might progress as follows:

> Your account, with a past-due balance of $398.75, has just appeared in my "tickle file." That indicates it's time to tickle your memory with a reminder that you owe us some money.
>
> If you have already mailed your check, please accept my thanks. We look forward to being able to serve you again.
>
> •
>
> There is probably a good reason why you haven't answered our inquiries about your overdue account of $398.75. Sometimes a statement is misfiled, a check is lost in the mail, or there is an error in our records. Whatever the source of the problem, we are in the dark until we hear from you.
>
> We have two reasons for wanting a response. Obviously, we want to be paid. But just as important, we want you to feel free to reorder. By clearing your account now, you will allow us to continue sending you the supplies you need, as you need them. That will help your sales—and ours. Why not check your inventory and use the enclosed envelope to send an order along with your payment?
>
> •

Your company and ours may have something in common: a cash flow problem. In our case, the problem comes from customers who don't pay their bills. Is that the source of your difficulty, too? The ripple effect from slow-paying customers makes us realize how we are all in this boat together; when each of us does our share of the rowing, it helps everyone to get ashore.

Your past-due balance is $398.75. If special circumstances make complete payment impossible, please let us know so that we can work out a schedule of reduced installments. You have been a valued customer, and we want to keep it that way.

•

When all else fails, you drop back 20 and punt. That pretty well describes our situation. You have not answered our previous letters, reminding you of your now long-past-due balance of $398.75.

This leaves us no alternative but to "punt," by referring your account to the Friendly Collection Agency. We consider this a drastic step, so we are writing one more time to ask your cooperation. Your prompt action will stop us from pursuing a course we would rather avoid; it will also protect your good name. Please let us hear from you by May 10th.

Creditors have better memories than debtors.
— *Ben Franklin,* in *Poor Richard's Almanac*

RAINBOW GLASS AND MIRROR CO.

300 CORTLAND AVENUE   SAN FRANCISCO, CALIFORNIA 94110   (415) 824-3000

November 4, 1990

Mr. Timothy L. Lathrop
Lathrop Plumbing Supply, Inc.
140 Lathrop Avenue
Lathrop, Kentucky 48059

Dear Mr. Lathrop:

Thank you for your prompt response to our request for payment of Invoice No. 7304. We reviewed our books and bank deposits once again to see if your check was incorrectly entered but could find no record of it.

By now the bank should have returned the cancelled check to you. Will you please send us a photocopy of both sides? I enclose a self-addressed, stamped envelope for your convenience.

If you are unable to find the cancelled check, then we must assume your payment was lost in the mails. In that case, you might use the enclosed envelope to send us a new check.

I appreciate your help in resolving this matter.

Sincerely yours,

Linda D. Green
Controller

jkd

Enclosure: Envelope

Sample Collection Letter written in Semiblock format.

Sales Letters

Sales letters are the life blood of most companies. Many rely entirely on direct mail to bring in new business. Some include letters as one part of a multifaceted marketing program. But few are able to conduct an effective sales effort without counting on letters as one of the important ways to make customers aware of their products.

To write an effective sales letter, you should focus both on the product and on its market. Think carefully about the nature of the product or service in terms of its appeal to a particular market. List the features of the product and then match them with the different kinds of buyer you will address. The result will be a group of letters, each describing the same product but stressing the aspects you consider to be of most interest to a particular customer. (Chapter 2, p. 31, discusses the AIDA formula for sales letters and how to analyze your readers.)

The following group of letters illustrates how you can "pitch" the same service, an insurance program, to different markets.

•

(To The Young Family)

> Insurance is a gamble . . . between you and the insurance company. But there's one thing that's a pretty sure bet. You're paying too much for the coverage you have. There's no need to pay maxi-dollars to get maxi-protection for your growing family. You can have the same protection at far less cost than most insurance agents would have you believe.

> At ABC Financial Services, an insurance program is tailored to your situation, whatever your income or goals. Yet it covers all the important elements of an insurance package: emergency funds, inflation, retirement, disability, or death.

> Give us a call at 665-7000. We want to help you keep the lid on the cost of living.

•

(To The Homemaker)

Planning meals is a lot like planning your budget—both
need to be well balanced. That's why ABC Financial
Services has a diversified program to cover all the important
financial considerations: emergency funds, retirement,
inflation, disability or death.

Regardless of your age or income, we can develop a plan
that fits your situation and responds to your financial goals.

Give us a call at 665-7000. We'll be glad to give you more
information or find a convenient time to talk to you about
our program.

•

(To The Sports Enthusiast)

Monday morning quarterbacking just won't do when it
comes to planning your family's financial future. You have
to cover too many bases:
— emergency funds
— retirement
— inflation
— disability/death

That's why ABC Financial Services has a diversified
program that is both systematic and flexible. It can be
tailored to your income, your age, and your expectations.

Give us a call, We'll help plan a financial program to assure
your having the money you need, when you need it.

•

Insurance companies play the odds. But you don't have to, in order to get maximum coverage at minimum cost.

Chances are, you're paying too much. At ABC Financial Services we will develop an insurance program for your particular situation—whatever your income or goals—at far less cost than your present program. Yet it will cover the essentials:

GUARANTEED INCOME–Available for emergencies;

GROWTH–Putting your money to work to keep up with inflation;

PROTECTION–Financial support in the event of death or disability.

A call to 665-7000 is all that's needed to start you down the road to big savings in insurance coverage.

•

Does your nest egg keep getting nibbled?
Do you think you're too young to start planning for retirement?
Would major hospital bills or disability wipe you out?
Does inflation seem remote—like a problem that affects only senior citizens?

If "Yes" is your answer to any of those questions, you should know about ABC Financial Services.

We start where you are— whatever your age or income— and develop a financial plan that is surprisingly simple and inexpensive. Yet it covers all the major money problems you are likely to encounter.

A call to 665-7000 will set up an appointment at your convenience.

•

The Downtown Health Club

1466 Main Street, Tucson, Arizona 80499

Telephone (123) 123-1122

January 20, 1990

Mr. Everett T. Tobias
1495 Century Plaza, 11th Floor
Tucson, Arizona 80499

DOWNTOWN HEALTH CLUB OPENS

Have you ever noticed how people who survive a heart attack
suddenly start watching their diet and getting exercise?
There's a reason. Their bodies have finally succeeded in
sending them a message.

Now a heart attack is a compelling way to get your attention,
but it's also a risky one. It's smart to get the message
without having the heart attack.

The message is clear: Regular exercise and a sound diet
improve the quality--and length--of our lives.

We all know it, but many of us put off doing anything about it.
The new Downtown Health Club will change that. Our extended
hours and convenient location allow complete flexibility in
scheduling exercise breaks at any time of the day or evening.

And what does Downtown offer to members? Fully equipped exercise rooms, a swimming pool, jacuzzi, sauna, steam rooms, and
handball courts; regularly scheduled classes and private
instruction. We also provide consultation with nutritionists
and a follow-up Diet Watch. Truly a comprehensive program!

During the month of February, we're offering a free trial week
to certain prospective members. We're sure that's all the time
you will need to decide the Downtown way to health and fitness
works.

The enclosed brochure tells you more about our facilities and
the various types of membership. Give us a try. You'll be
doing your heart a favor.

ANTHONY JACKSON
VICE PRESIDENT, MEMBERSHIP

Sample Sales Letter written in Simplified Letter format.

Letters of Recommendation

A letter recommending a friend or an employee for a job should include the following information:

- how long you have known the individual,
- the nature of your acquaintance or relationship (e.g., supervisor, classmate),
- your evaluation of the individual's qualifications.

In writing the letter, consider that it may be read by the person it describes. This may crimp your frankness a bit, but it is safer in the long run.

The amount of detail you provide will reveal your level of enthusiasm about the candidate; a few generalized statements will suggest a satisfactory performance, but paragraphs of meaningful description will indicate that you believe the candidate possesses superior qualifications.

The following letter provides a strong recommendation:

> Cynthia Llewellyn has worked directly under my supervision for the past seven years. Her assignments concerning the geophysics and chemistry of manganese nodules called for a grasp of the fundamental problems as well as meticulous attention to detail. Ms. Llewellyn has proved to be industrious, conscientious, and skillful in carrying out her assignments.
>
> During the course of her work, Ms. Llewellyn developed software that expedited the job of converting raw data into useful form; she calibrated our sedimentometer and used it to measure systems of interest. She has had experience in zonal rotor work on the Epson B-2000 ultracentrifuge and has used the Ellery 21 spectrophotometer extensively. Her recent work in electron microscopy stimulated a new line of research.
>
> Ms. Llewellyn has a high degree of integrity and a cheerful personality. Her intellectual vigor and the tenacity with which she has pursued her work in our laboratory suggest that she is well qualified to participate in a program leading to the Ph.D. degree.

BUSCAGLIA BROTHERS PUBLISHING

Since 1895

May 14, 1990

Ms. Sandra O'Shea
Peters Publishing
1028 Avenue of the Americas
New York, New York 10022

Dear Ms. O'Shea:

Maria Nelson has been my secretary for eight years. I will
indeed be sorry to lose her services when she moves to New
York next month. But I agree with her decision and feel
she is the right person for the position she is seeking with
your company.

Ms. Nelson is one of those rare individuals who can both
follow instructions and take initiative, as appropriate.
She is a productive contributor to team efforts as well as
a self-starter.

Her competence extends beyond the secretarial skills for
which she was originally hired; her talent for organization
has changed our files from a source of frustration and lost
documents to a genuine information retrieval system. She is
equally strong in time management.

Ms. Nelson demonstrated her willingness and ability to take
on a challenge when we installed a word processing system.
She put in many hours on her own, studying manuals and
mastering the system's somewhat complex capabilities.

Seldom have I been able to make such an unqualified recommendation regarding an employee. I have no hesitation in
advising you to hire her.

Very truly yours,

Joseph P. Buscaglia

Joseph P. Buscaglia

1000 CHERRY LANE, SAN CARLOS, CALIFORNIA 94070 / PHONE (415) 595-0404

Sample Letter of Recommendation in Full Block format.

Job Application Letters and Résumés

The line between resumes and letters of application is fuzzy. Sometimes a letter incorporates the kind of detail found in a resume, and thus performs both functions. Other letters are designed to accompany a resume which contains most of the pertinent information. In either case, the job application letter may be one of the most important letters you will write in your lifetime; it deserves your careful attention.

Most of your attention should be directed toward winnowing out the detail that will interest a prospective employer. People are usually busy; they don't want to spend time searching through a mountain of irrelevant detail for the nuggets of information they need. Simplify the job for them by focusing your letter or resume on the aspects of your experience that bear on their particular problems. Move into the employer's shoes, examining your background not from the standpoint of "This is what I have done," but "Here is how I can help you."

Make a list of your accomplishments, using action verbs to describe them. If possible, show the results of what you did, not a laundry list of activities or job functions. For example:

> Achieved 15% capture rate on proposals to business and government clients.

> Instituted and directed a marketing contact scheme which doubled our list of active customers.

Where appropriate, list specific skills, such as the ability to operate certain equipment or apparatus. It helps if you provide a lead-in that underscores the significance of your list. For example:

> The following employment history demonstrates my range of skills and adaptability to a variety of situations. I bring to each task talents for organizing, learning quickly, synthesizing, and communicating well.

If you have only limited job experience, or none at all, consider what you *do* have to offer a potential employer. With a little imagination you may find you have just what an employer needs. For example, here's a letter looking for that magical first job:

If you are looking for summer help this year, I would like you to consider hiring me. It won't cost you much money, since my rates are low. But at the same time, I will do a good job for you, because I am quick to learn and eager to please.

I have some mailroom experience, a California driver's license, and I'm six feet tall, so I can reach high places. I could perform many useful tasks—run errands, file, do library research, handle simple repair jobs, to name a few.

My abilities are indicated by a 3.5 grade point average (I'm a senior at City High School, graduating in June), and by my earning a general ham radio license at the age of 15. I would really like to turn those capabilities into experience.

I will give you a call soon to find out if I can help your company this summer. Thank you for your consideration.

A resume should contain the following information:

- Name, address, telephone number
- Job objective
- Education
- Thumbnail description of relevant qualifications in narrative form
- Employment history
- References (or statement that references will be supplied on request)

It should be brief and, above all, should have a pleasing appearance. A messy resume or one that is difficult to read is a poor reflection on your interest in the company.

If your letter accompanies a resume, add enough detail to make the recipient want to read the resume. For example:

The enclosed resume will give you a quick glimpse of my qualifications for temporary work with your firm. I am available for short- or long-term projects, working in your office or at my home where I have an IBM Selectric typewriter and drafting equipment.

You will find that my rates are attractive in comparison with those of temporary agencies, and my proximity to your office adds flexibility. Most important, my varied background and capabilities will make me a valuable resource for your company.

I would be happy to expand on my qualifications and discuss your temporary employment needs in person.

•

If your letter does not enclose a resume, include only enough information to arouse interest in your qualifications. The goal of the letter is to obtain a job interview, where you can provide additional details. The following letters include some resume-type information but do not attempt to replace the resume:

Today's *Tribune* indicates an opening in your Marketing Department. I believe the initiative and enthusiasm I would bring to such a position will be of interest to you.

In my ten years in sales, I have demonstrated an unusual ability to find new markets and to develop novel applications for existing products. For example:

- I inaugurated and supervised a complete direct mail program, including preparation of the mailing pieces, selection of the mailing list, and analysis of the returns; the exceptional 5% response rate to our mailing made direct mail a standard part of the company's marketing plans.

- I developed the market for a line of books in quick-print shops; the high sales volume resulting from the close match between the books and the interests of the shops' clientele led to nationwide distribution through several printshop franchises.

- I supervised the design and staffing of a trade show booth that produced nearly twice as many sales leads as previous trade shows.

No letter can adequately convey an individual's talents. If my background resembles the qualifications you are seeking, I feel certain a personal interview would be worthwhile.

•

Turnover is often a problem in a medical office staff. That's why you may be interested in my background in hospital recordkeeping—and my tenacity.

I have worked more than 5,000 hours as a volunteer at Harbor Hospital. My responsibilities included bookkeeping for the hospital gift shop (paying suppliers, recording sales, and transferring profits monthly to the hospital), and sorting over 600 pieces of patient mail each week.

I have a working knowledge of the forms required by insurance companies and by various governmental agencies, based on assistance I have rendered to my elderly parents and to a number of their friends.

My interest in working in a doctor's office has prompted me to study medical terminology on my own. If part of your employee screening procedures includes testing in this area, I believe you will find I have pursued my studies well.

My family-raising years are now behind me, and I am looking forward to a couple of productive decades in medical office work. If it appears that I can provide the kind of help you need, I would be pleased to meet with you.

Letters of Resignation

Retirement, accepting a better position, or job dissatisfaction are typical circumstances that call for a letter of resignation. Often such letters merely document an event that has been expected or discussed by all parties. A single sentence may suffice for this situation.

Please accept my resignation, effective November 1, 1990.

You may wish to include information or express sentiments beyond this bare-bones statement, however. The function of the letter should determine its tone and content. For example, if maintaining strong ties with the company you are leaving is important, your letter should be friendly.

It is with mixed feelings that I submit my resignation as Regional Sales Manager for Dynamo Builders. Because of the confidence you have shown in my ability to take on new assignments, my eleven years with the company have been a time of growth and challenge.

But as you know, for some time I have wanted to gain additional experience in other areas of marketing. I now have that opportunity and will be leaving Dynamo on March 15th.

I appreciate the support and encouragement you have given me during the years we have worked together.

Still other letters of resignation are the vehicle for documenting grievances. Even if you intend to publish your letter in the local newspaper, however, a tone of objectivity is appropriate.

By this letter I am resigning my position as Deputy District Attorney, effective immediately. In the five years I have served as prosecutor, I have attempted to correct the imbalance in our system of justice that favors the criminal over the victim. You and I have frequently debated the role of the District Attorney's office in this endeavor but have seldom agreed.

I have concluded that I can no longer function as a prosecutor when the policies followed by the present administration fail to provide the support I need to obtain convictions.

March 28, 1912

Mr. Rupert S. Murray, Chairman
White Star Steamship Company
Pier 37
Liverpool

Dear Mr. Murray:

This letter puts into writing the resignation I regretfully
submitted to you in person yesterday. I feel the greatest
loyalty to the company and wish to express my gratitude
for the encouragement given to me throughout the years
of my advancement from Cabin Boy to Chief Engineer.

As you know, I had planned to retire following my next tour
of duty at sea. However, the personal circumstances we
discussed make it impossible for me to assume those duties
when the ship sails next week. It therefore seems appropriate
to move the date of retirement forward to April 1, 1912,
to correspond to the present situation.

My regret concerning this action is all the stronger for my
being unable to participate in the maiden voyage of the
newest in a long line of illustrious passenger ships. I had
been looking forward to having my final tour on "the engineer-
ing marvel of the century." Although I will be unable to be
on board, my spirit will be with the Titanic when she sails
from Liverpool next week.

With my sincere thanks,

Oliver P. Dewhurst

5
Personal Letters

CHAPTER 5
Personal Letters

Though telephones and long-distance travel have changed some of the ways we communicate, letters continue to be an important means of conducting personal affairs. They allow us to:

- express thanks or sympathy,
- share experiences,
- register a complaint,
- make views known to elected officials,
- extend an invitation,
- maintain friendships over long distances.

The irony is that while everyone likes to receive letters, few of us take the time to write them. We use lack of time as an excuse, when the truth is that we are just not comfortable putting words on paper. The art of writing personal letters has been allowed to lapse.

Your letter will thus be more powerful than ever. If you write to a company protesting their advertising policies, you will be heard. If you write to a newspaper editor presenting a point of view, your letter will probably be published. A well-written letter makes people sit up and take notice.

A letter is also an excellent way to express your feelings. When a friend experiences a death in the family or is seriously ill, a letter is one of the most meaningful ways to show you care. Sharing good feelings is equally important—the joy of becoming a grandparent, the excitement of travel, the fun of a class reunion. The contact we maintain through letters can be a haven in an impersonal world.

This chapter includes samples of the kinds of letters you might want to write. They are not formulas to be followed, but suggestions for the form or spirit of specific types of letters; your own thoughts will provide more appropriate words for a particular situation. In most circumstances, the key ingredient is the sincerity with which you express yourself.

> *A short letter to a distant friend is, in my opinion, an insult like that of a slight bow or cursory salutation—a proof of unwillingness to do much, even where there is a necessity of doing something.*
> —Samuel Johnson

To Type or Not To Type

The most personal of letters, such as letters of sympathy, thanks, and congratulations, should always be handwritten. Letters to government officials, newspaper editors, or to businesses will probably produce the best results if they are typewritten. With other letters, you may follow your own inclinations.

Typing a letter to a friend is no longer considered a social blunder. Family members will receive more news in less of your time when you type letters to them. But if your mood is more suited to curling up with pen and paper than sitting down to a keyboard, by all means write by hand. The more you enjoy the letter-writing process, the better your letter will be.

Letters to
Family and Friends

The format of personal letters is quite simple. Put the date near the top of the page, usually on the right side. No inside address is used. Place a comma following the salutation, instead of the colon used in business letters. Indent paragraphs about an inch, if handwritten, or five spaces, if typed. That's about all there is to it.

Sympathy

For some, the most difficult letters are those expressing sympathy. You may feel awkward about communicating emotions to someone who has suffered the loss of a loved one, and you hesitate to write for fear that the words you choose will be clumsy or inadequate. But remember, many people feel this way; as a result, the person experiencing grief may be cut off from much-needed support. Reaching out with a few carefully chosen words is a very human thing to do.

The letter need not be long. If you are not a close friend or member of the family, a couple of sentences will suffice. In all cases, a few handwritten words will mean more than a purchased card.

The news of your loss has saddened both of us. We send you our sympathy at this difficult time.

•

It was with sadness that I learned of your wife's death. Please accept my sincere condolences.

When you had a close relationship with the deceased, sharing your thoughts and feelings can be a comfort to the family. Anecdotes that reveal the person's character are welcomed as a way to keep alive the memory of the loved one.

Michael's death came as a tragic shock. Few seemed more full of life than he, making the loss all the more keenly felt by us all. Mike was one of the most mature young men I have known. He always knew the right thing to do, and he put everyone at ease with his friendly, natural manner. He could usually find something to laugh about, including his own mistakes; he was never guilty of taking himself too seriously.

This period of learning to live with Michael's death will be difficult for you. We will miss him too, but he is very much alive in the memory of all of us who knew him. Our sympathies are with you.

•

Your letter came as a message of sweet sorrow. Sweet for reminding us of the many times spent with your parents, always joyful and rewarding, full of happiness. Sorrow, but for a moment, for the loss of immediate contact with ones so dear.

We send our blessings to your families, whose lives were so enriched by the parenthood of Charles and Evelyn.

When death comes in later years, your letter can mention the long, full life of the person. When an infant or child dies, your letter would usually acknowledge the loss felt by the parents. For example:

While no word of mine can ease your loss, I want you to know that you are in my thoughts and heart at this time of sorrow.

Letters of sympathy reflect the character and beliefs of the person writing them. Obviously, you should not use the occasion to try to convert the recipient to a particular point of view, but you should feel free to express yourself in religious terms if those are the words that come to you naturally. Divergence of religious beliefs is unimportant when the desire to console is sincere.

Response to Sympathy Letter

A brief note is usually sent in response to expressions of sympathy. A few lines are all that is needed.

> Thank you for being so thoughtful. Letters such as yours have meant a great deal to me at this time.

•

> Your memories of my father were a source of great joy to me. Thank you for sharing them with me.

Thank-You Notes

Letters saying "thank you" should be written for many occasions. When you receive a gift or are someone's guest, when you are granted an interview or given a reference—any time you have been the beneficiary of someone's hospitality, generosity, or willingness to help, a note of thanks is appropriate.

The letter should be written promptly; allowing a long interval to elapse casts doubt on the sincerity of your appreciation. The letter need not be long, but the most meaningful expression of thanks will identify the occasion for your gratitude. A "bread and butter" letter might be written as follows:

> My visit to Chicago was a memorable occasion, made all the more so by your thoughtful hospitality. You certainly know how to make a guest feel at home! Your delicious meals were a treat, and your flexibility in adapting to my irregular schedule made many things possible.
>
> I hope your travels will soon bring you our way. Plan on staying with us, and we will look forward to more hours of stimulating discussion—and just plain fun.

MEGALOPOLIS UNIVERSITY
3700 West Juniper Boulevard
Atlanta, Georgia 54321

Office of The Dean of Students   Telephone (123) 333-9999

November 15, 1990

Dear David,

Tom and I both want to thank you for the many kindnesses
you showed Mark when he visited your campus last weekend.
He has returned full of enthusiasm for Handler College.
Having been raised in the shadow of a large university,
he found the close contact between students and faculty
at Handler particularly exciting.

You were right on target to arrange an interview with
Dr. Tolstad of the Physics Department and to have a
student take Mark to a soccer game. Seeing the well-
equipped laboratories and the spirit of the athletes
confirmed his belief that he has chosen the right school.

If you will be in our area in the coming months, do give
us a call. We would enjoy having you come for dinner
and an evening of catching up. Give Ellen our regards.

                              Cordially,

                              Kimberly Marshall

Dr. David R. Hodges
Office of the President
Handler College
Simpkins, North Carolina 25739

Sample Thank-You Letter written in Official format.

Buying a commercial card is never as satisfactory a way of expressing your thanks as a few handwritten sentences. The emotions you are conveying are supposed to be your own, not those of the greeting card company.

When you have received a gift, you should mention it in your note and briefly allude to how useful it is or how pleased you are to have it.

Diane and I appreciate your thoughtful choice of wedding present. The salad bowl will not only be useful, but it's a real beauty as well. We're working hard on our long-hidden talents as gourmet cooks, and the bowl will be a pleasure to have for our culinary creations. Thanks from both of us!

•

The dictionary you sent arrived today. You have probably noticed that my spelling could stand some improvement, and there is no doubt that the dictionary will see a great deal of use when I get to college. My thanks for picking out such a helpful gift.

•

Even when you are not particularly thrilled with a gift, a brief note is in order. You may not be able to express yourself quite as sincerely as you would if you liked the gift, but keep in mind that it was sent with the best of intentions, and you can probably find something to say.

What a conversation piece the door knocker is! We are especially pleased to have a memento of your travels in India and appreciate your effort in bringing it back. Many thanks.

Travel

When you are able to travel to interesting places, writing to friends or relatives allows you to share your experiences with them. Too often, however, letters describing a trip are not much more than an itinerary—a list of cities and countries visited. Your reader would probably rather hear some anecdotes of your adventures, or your reaction to what you have seen. You needn't cover the whole trip—just those aspects you think would be of most interest to a particular reader. For example:

> Greetings from Switzerland! This country has certainly lived up to all the advance reports—the scenery is every bit as spectacular as it looks in the picture books. Switzerland is also my candidate for the cleanest country in the world. Every house and yard is immaculate. Land is too valuable to let junk accumulate on it; it is all put to good use, for people or animals.
>
> One of the most common uses is to grow vegetables and flowers. Every house has its vegetable garden; we even saw vegetables being grown between the tracks on a railroad siding! And every house where we have been guests had fresh flowers on the table, even though it's winter. Perhaps the gray weather at this time of year makes the addition of some bright colors a virtual necessity. Whatever the reason, I am impressed by the year-round fresh-flower habit of the Swiss.

To Your Children

Over the centuries, parents have used letters to advise their children—to study hard, resist temptations, make them proud, avoid bad companions, take care of their health—and to write home! Mail from home is usually welcomed, but not if it turns out to be a lecture in longhand. Such letters are often ineffective. For example, Lady Churchill wrote to her 15-year-old son:

> Darling Winston,
> I hope you will try and not smoke. If only you knew how foolish and silly you look doing it you would give it up ...

Letters can be one of the best ways to hold a family together over long distances; they do that job best when you use them to share your thoughts and show your affection.

> There's a large hole now when the family gathers around the dinner table each evening. It's amazing how easy it is to take someone for granted, until they are no longer here. Well, any question about how much you added by your presence has been erased by your absence —lots!
>
> Some things don't change. I still beat your father at Scrabble, and he still falls asleep while reading the evening paper. Your brother has some part of his anatomy bandaged at all times, and loses his homework at least once a week. The peach tree is blooming in the backyard now, but I really knew spring was well underway when Dad hauled out the lawnmower last weekend. It made me realize that summer will soon be here, and so will you. Good luck with exams—cookies will shortly be on their way to help you through the ordeal.

•

As Consumer and Citizen

You have the power to influence corporations and Congress; one of the best ways to exercise that influence is by writing letters.

Your letters will be most effective if they are directed to an individual. The reference librarian at your local library can probably help with names and addresses of corporate officers or elected officials.

Letters of Complaint

Consumer attitudes and satisfaction are carefully monitored by most companies. If you have cause for complaint—sloppy workmanship, unsatisfactory service, or objectionable advertising policies, for example—speak up about it. Draw up an outline of your case before you start writing; facts and emotions often become tangled if you don't first sort them out. You may be boiling mad, but unless you make it clear to your reader why you are angry, you may be treated as "just another crank." Putting the reader on the defensive will not further your cause. Express your complaint or anger responsibly, assuming that the reader is intelligent and wants to hear your views.

> As president of Cleanmore Manufacturing Company, you are undoubtedly interested in the consumer's view of your products and service. I have been a Cleanmore buyer for more than 20 years and have always found your appliances to perform satisfactorily; in fact, I never had to think about them. That is why my problems with a washer that I recently purchased have been such an unpleasant surprise. A copy of the receipt is enclosed, to identify the model number and date of purchase.
>
> Less than three months after I purchased the washer, it started overflowing, creating a major cleanup problem in the kitchen. Since it was well within the guarantee period, I requested repairs. The serviceman who arrived said he would have to return with a replacement part for the control panel; it was two weeks before he returned. The

machine operated satisfactorily for one month and then started overflowing again.

This time the service department took three weeks to respond; when the service rep arrived, he once again did not have the part needed. Further delays pushed his return housecall past the warranty period. You can imagine my shock when I received a bill for $138 for this "service." My protests that the service department delays were the reason the machine was no longer under warranty were politely rejected. At least they were polite. But that doesn't diminish my anger over such unfair treatment.

I believe in going right to the top when I have a problem. I am therefore writing to ask for your help in correcting what surely must be an improper interpretation of your warranty.

•

The aim of advertising is to sell a product. Why, then, has your company created an ad campaign that insults the intelligence of your potential market?

Your current ads for the SX-47 sportcar all but guarantee that, if I drive it, I will have a dozen gorgeous girlfriends—at least until your next model comes out. For myself, I prefer to rely on other means for enjoying social interaction.

When I'm shopping for a car, I want to know what its repair record is like, what mileage it gets, how it holds up under stress, how fast it depreciates, and whether its design allows me to perform routine maintenance. I'd like to know how many suitcases it will hold, not how many Playboy bunnies.

Consumers are increasingly well educated, and we are less willing to spend money for short-term kicks. At a time when domestic car manufacturers are working hard to keep their customers, you would do well to appeal to the discerning buyer.

I assume that your car has merits other than sex appeal. Please tell us what they are.

•

Soliciting Funds

Organizations and schools often take to the mails to raise money for their continued existence. If you are called upon to write such a letter, keep it short and make it as convincing and interesting as you can. You have a lot of competition in the mailbox, so it takes a careful choice of words and maybe even a sense of humor to make your letter stand out.

•

In today's economy, it's hard to know what a dollar is worth. Our sense of the salary we deserve, or the amount of rent it's reasonable to pay, becomes increasingly distorted.

In such times, it is helpful to reorder our priorities around what we value most—things that may have previously been considered intangibles, like clean air, good health, and a sense that we have a contribution to make.

The Healthful Air Group (HAG) is made up of people like yourself who have banded together to increase their clout with regard to a crucial issue. Unclean air means poor health and low spirits, and without our health, how can we enjoy the other delights life has to offer?

As a contributor to HAG, you will be supporting a successful lobbying effort and public awareness campaign that could well change the quality of your own life. The enclosed brochure describes HAG's programs and how you can help in this important movement.

•

Lie still now, and let me drop some water on your forehead. At least that may seem to be what I'm doing with my annual reminder to classmates of the need to support Ivy College. But it frequently seems to require repetition to produce action—and action may be appropriate with regard to disposition of your worldly goods.

If you haven't reviewed your will for a number of years, you might be surprised to see how quickly it has become outdated. Or, if you have never taken the time to write your will, there's no better time than right now, while your faculties are still in reasonably good working order.

In any event, may I urge you to consider including some form of allocation for Ivy in your planning. Did you realize that you can contribute to Ivy and receive a tax benefit that can make money? The enclosed brochure suggests some possibilities. In these times when so many of us are looking for value received for our contributions, the quality education that Ivy continues to provide looks like more and more of a bargain.

We have now been associated with Ivy College for nearly one-third of its 90 years. The investment we made in our education has continued to provide a variety of dividends over the years. Remembering Ivy in our estate planning can help assure that others will have a similar opportunity.

•

Letters to Government Representatives

Government representatives, including the President, pay attention to the *quantity* of mail they receive regarding a specific bill or legislative problem. They record the "Yeas" and "Nays" to indicate public sentiment in their constituency, and your letter is tallied in one or the other column.

But elected representatives are often more interested in the *quality* of the letters they receive. Form letters sent by members of an organization, even though they may be individually typed or handwritten,

May 15, 1990

Honorable Sheila Sorensen
Senator, 37th District
State Capitol Building
Sacramento, CA 95814

Dear Ms. Sorensen:

I want to thank you for your continued support of the
State Scholarship Program. During the past ten years,
just such financial aid as you voted for last month has
helped each of my three children earn bachelor's degrees.
Without the state's help, they would have been forced
to delay their studies while they earned the money
for tuition and books.

I believe that the scholarship program is a sound investment
of state funds, even in these times of tight budgets. My
children, and thousands of others like them whose families
could not meet the high cost of a college education, are
now productive citizens. Their educations allow them
to contribute in many ways to their communities, to
earn higher incomes—and to pay more taxes!

I hope you and your colleagues who voted funds for this
year's scholarship program will continue to be in the
majority, so that other promising students can be helped.

Very truly yours,

Grace Collins

Grace Collins

Sample Letter to Elected Representative
(Block Style)

114

are merely counted. But a carefully written letter that expresses an individual's view is pulled from the huge stack of mail received each week and given special attention. Such letters may be the only ones actually read by the senator or representative, while assistants handle the rest.

Your letters should observe the following rules to be most effective:

- Make the letter short; no more than one page, if possible.
- Either type the letter or use legible longhand.
- Research the issue; if appropriate, identify legislation by name, number, and sponsors.
- Briefly explain the reasons behind your position—how a bill might create problems or alleviate them.
- Indicate the action you want taken.
- Be helpful rather than threatening; hostility is counter-productive. Offer to provide more information on a subject, if appropriate.
- Include your return address.
- Spell the representative's name correctly, and be sure to use the right address.

Your local reference librarian will provide the addresses you need and help you to identify a bill. You may address your letter to *Dear Senator, Dear Congresswoman,* or *Dear Congressman,* rather than using the very formal *Honorable* or *Most Honorable.* Sign your letter by hand.

> The Social Security Reform Bill, S999, will soon be coming to a vote in the Senate. I urge your support of this much needed legislation.
>
> Those of us on fixed incomes have a special interest in this bill. We are aware that changes in the system are needed to reflect the changing population—more of us are living longer. S999 appropriately corrects the system to reflect the needs of this older population. It also removes the limitation on earned income that has made it so difficult for us to keep up with the cost of living.
>
> Please give a "Yes" vote on S999 your serious consideration. Thank you.

6
Dear Sir or Madam

CHAPTER 6

Dear Sir or Madam

For generations, masculine terms have been used to indicate both sexes. Today, however, you will offend some people if you start a letter with *Dear Sir,* and many of your female readers will feel excluded if you write "The effective salesman wants his customers to be satisfied." To ignore these sensitivities is unwise, regardless of your views on the subject.

It is surprisingly easy to avoid sexist terms—simply acknowledging the problem is an important first step. You do not have to use language that is awkward or silly to avoid offending your readers. But using a good substitute for *Dear Sir* or *Gentlemen* improves the likelihood of your having a sympathetic audience.

A detailed exploration of sexist terms and their social implications is beyond the scope of *Better Letters*. The goal here is to review some of the alternatives currently being considered and adopted.

The following pages suggest ways to avoid trouble spots in your letters. As you develop new habits, you may find that nonsexist writing is actually better writing.

Social Titles
and Salutations

When Addressing Women

Mrs., *Miss*, and *Ms.* are abbreviations that tend to evoke strong responses. Most younger women prefer to be addressed either as *Ms.* or simply by their name without a title. Some women feel they have earned the right to put *Mrs.* in front of their name and enjoy being "branded" with their husband's name. Still others are proud to be *Miss* and want no part of the marital uncertainty of *Ms.*

Whenever such a preference is known, honor it. The easiest way to determine a preference is to notice how a woman signs her letters. If a preference is not known, either use *Ms.* or eliminate the social title.

Ms. Audrey Barnett	Audrey Barnett
1234 Main Street	1234 Main Street
Everytown, AM 56789	Everytown, AM 56789
Dear Ms. Barnett:	Dear Audrey Barnett:

Academic or professional titles always take precedence over social or courtesy titles. Their nonsexist nature makes them especially useful.

Dr. Phyllis Cohen	Senator Ellen Moss
Dear Dr. Cohen:	Dear Senator Moss:

When Addressing Individuals of Unknown Gender

Some first names are given to both men and women (e.g., Leslie, Lee, Jan, Kim, Casey). Some women use initials when signing their names (e.g., J.G. Wright). In such cases where you may be uncertain about gender, the custom of using *Mr.* is no longer appropriate. Instead, one possibility is to eliminate the social title and write the full name.

Dear Leslie Standish:	Dear J.G. Wright:

Another approach recommended by some handbooks is to abbreviate all social titles *(Mr., Mrs., Miss,* or *Ms.)* with the single letter *M.* The above examples would then become:

Dear M. Standish:	Dear M. Wright:

When the Addressee is Unknown

Any handbook that advises using *Dear Sir* or *Gentlemen* when you don't know your addressee's name is badly out of date. The modern equivalent of that advice is to write *Dear Sir or Madam, Gentlemen and Ladies,* or the reverse order. However, these substitutes are cumbersome and somewhat offensive. *Gentlepeople* and *Gentlepersons* have also been suggested, but they draw attention to themselves and invite ridicule. The quaint flavor of *To Whom It May Concern* is out of step with today's letter-writing language.

A variety of substitutes for outmoded salutations are presented in the following paragraphs.

Generic Title: Certain categories of addressee lend themselves to grouping under a generic title:

Dear Homeowner	Dear Contributor	Dear Executive
Dear Parents	Dear Employee	Dear Solar Enthusiast
Dear Customer	Dear Supplier	Dear Union Member

Job titles are sometimes used:

> Dear Credit Manager
>
> Dear Registrar
>
> Dear Editor

Some people prefer to repeat the name of the company:

> Dear Periwinkle Press
>
> Dear General Motors
>
> Dear Standard Pipe & Fixture Company

It may seem awkward to use the word *Dear* with a company name or job title. General Motors or Credit Managers are not "dear" to most people writing to them.

Generalized Salutation: Another approach eliminates the word *Dear* by using a greeting you might exchange in person. *Good Morning* is a favorite with some writers but has the inherent drawback that it may be inappropriate if the letter is read in the afternoon. *Hello* is popular with others but may seem too chummy. *Greetings* is suitable for many occasions when the addressee's name is unknown; however, the word *Greetings* may produce unpleasant connotations if the recipient has ever received a draft notice.

The choice of salutation is largely one of personal preference or suitability. If none of the suggested wordings seem exactly right, the best approach may be to eliminate the salutation altogether, as in memos or the Simplified Letter. (See Chapter 3.)

Memos: Although memos have been used for internal company communications for years, many people are now using the memo format for a variety of correspondence. A typical memo would start this way, flush with the left margin:

To: Sales Manager, Arctic Ice Chest Company

From: Nifty Insulation, Inc.

Date: January 15, 1990

Subject: Improving Your Products

(Text begins here)

Simplified Letters: Perhaps the Simplified Letter is the best solution when your addressee is unknown. It is more formal than a memo, while still eliminating the salutation. Here is an example of a letter written in the Simplified Letter format.

David Brothers
79 Wall Street
New Utopia, NW 25000

INSIDER TRADING

Recent criminal charges have focused national attention on investment bankers and other "insiders" who buy and sell stock on the basis of proprietary information. As members of the New Utopia Stock Exchange, we must each police our own firm to wipe out this unethical—and illegal—practice.

The integrity of the entire industry is at stake. Clients are asking if we can be trusted with confidential information, and small investors see these cases as confirmation that the stock market is not for them.

We will be inviting unwanted government intervention if we are unable to control this practice. Self-regulation is the only solution. As a start, I urge you to adopt the measures suggested in the enclosed guidelines. Let me know your company's ideas for eliminating insider trading; I will include them in a follow-up letter next month.

BENJAMIN BROKER
PRESIDENT

When Addressing Couples

Today many married women retain their own last name or hyphenate their name with that of their husband. Some husbands also hyphenate their name with their wife's name. And many couples live together without being married, thus not changing their names.

Each of these situations may pose problems for the letter writer; however, you have some latitude in the arrangement and order of names. If you follow individual preferences when they are known, and common sense when a preference is not known, you will probably offend no one.

If the husband's name has been taken, the customary way to address the couple is:

> Mr. and Mrs. Charles Young
>
> (Dear Mr. and Mrs. Young)

If the woman prefers to use her first name, the correct form of address would be:

> Mr. Charles and Mrs. Deborah Young
>
> (Dear Mr. and Mrs. Young)

(Cases where one or both have professional titles are covered in Chapter 3, p. 59)

If the woman has retained her maiden name, and both last names are relatively short, they should be placed on the same line:

> Ms. Deborah Adams and Mr. Charles Young
>
> (Dear Ms. Adams and Mr. Young)

If the last names are too long for one line, put them on separate lines:

> Mr. Theodore Throckmorton
> Ms. Wilhelmina VonFurstenburg
>
> (Dear Mr. Throckmorton and Ms. Von Furstenburg)

Some etiquette authorities state that separate lines should also be used for the names of an unmarried couple living together; others handle the names as they would a married couple where the wife has retained her maiden name.

The order of names is either alphabetical or arbitrary, depending on which authority you consult. Alphabetical order seems to have the advantage of impartiality.

If a hyphenated name has been adopted, follow the usage of the individuals involved.

> Mr. and Mrs. Charles Adams-Young
>
> Mr. Charles Young and Mrs. Deborah Adams-Young

Problem Words

Man

Man demonstrates the changes in meaning a word can undergo. The Old English meaning of the word was "person" or "human being," and it was applied to either sex. Thus someone's daughter or sister or mother could be described as "a beautiful man." Eventually the word *man* ceased to be used with regard to individual women. It became a term that distinguished adult males from adult females while it continued to mean both sexes taken as a group—thereby producing some significant ambiguities.

Many women feel that using *man* as a word for people of both sexes relegates women to a second-class status. You may not share this view;

there is considerable precedent for using *man* to mean all human beings. But that will bring little consolation if insisting on using *man* in this general sense muddies your meaning or alienates your reader. You have other ways to express the concept.

Problem Word	Replacement
to man (verb), as in "to man the booth")	work, staff, run, operate
manpower	personnel, staff, workers
mankind	human beings, humanity, civilization, the human race
manmade	artificial, synthetic, handmade, machine-made
man-hour	work-hour
chairman	chairwoman, chairperson, chair
salesman	saleswoman, salesperson, sales rep
layman, laymen	layperson, laypeople
councilman	councilwoman, council member
congressman	congresswoman, member of Congress
Englishmen, Frenchmen	the English, the French
businessman	executive
repairman	service rep

Note that words like *chairman* and *congressman* are perfectly appropriate when used in connection with a specific male.

The following pairs of sentences illustrate some common uses of *man* and suggest alternative wordings. Notice how the ambiguity disappears when you do not have to guess whether *man* includes women.

Unemployment rates are meaningful to the average working man whose job may be on the line.

Unemployment rates are meaningful to the average worker (or wage earner) whose job may be on the line.

Pollsters rely on the opinion of the man in the street for their predictions.

Pollsters rely on the opinions of the average person (or voter) for their predictions.

•

Ancient man devised ways to observe the motions of the planets.

Our ancestors devised ways to observe the motions of the planets.

•

A man who lies needs a good memory.

A liar needs a good memory.—*Quintilian*

•

Man's creativity displays itself in . . .

Human creativity displays itself in . . .

•

Mankind owes to the child the best it has to give.
—*United Nations Declaration*

Humanity (or The human race) owes to the child the best it has to give.

•

I know of no rights of race superior to the rights of mankind.

I know of no rights of race superior to the rights of humanity.
—*Frederick Douglass*

A common misunderstanding is that we should avoid the syllable *man* wherever it occurs. This confusion created a national pastime as we dreamed up outrageous substitutes. *Personeuver, personhole,* and *persondolin* were typical results of this overdone exercise.

But the syllable *man* is not always derived from the Old English *man. Human* is from the Latin *humanus* (human being; man, as distinguished from the lower animals). Words such as *manipulate, manage, manufacture,* and *manuscript* are derived from the Latin *manus* (hand); they have no roots in common with our word *man* and present no problems of ambiguity. We do not need substitutes for the syllable *man,* just for the generic term.

Masculine Pronouns

He, him, and *his* are good words to indicate a male person or the masculine possessive. If you wish to refer to females as well, you have several currently acceptable options:

- Change from singular to plural,
- Use both pronouns,
- Write in the second person,
- Revise to eliminate masculine pronouns.

Change from singular to plural. This allows you to use the neutral pronouns *they, them,* and *their.* The following quotations illustrate this approach; they appear first in their original form and then changed to plural.

> Since a politician never believes what he says, he is always astonished when others do.—*Charles DeGaulle*

> Since politicians never believe what they say, they are always astonished when others do.

> I can remember way back when a liberal was one who was generous with his own money.—*Will Rogers*

> I can remember way back when liberals were the ones who were generous with their own money.

The plural pronoun *they* is often used in singular constructions. Although this is grammatically incorrect, the trend indicates the widespread desire to avoid using masculine pronouns for both sexes.

> It's enough to drive anyone out of their senses.—*G.B. Shaw*

Use both pronouns. If the plural form is not appropriate, you may prefer to write *he or she, her or his,* or *him or her.* In occasional use, the awkwardness of this construction is probably not a serious drawback. But repeated use suggests that you should rewrite to avoid these pronouns altogether. Some writers consolidate *she and he* to *s/he,* while others have coined neutral pronouns such as *co, un,* and *per.* Wide acceptance of one of these would solve the pronoun problem, but this does not appear to be imminent.

Write in the second person. In some circumstances you can address the reader as *you* (second person) rather than as the more anonymous *he, she,* or *they* (third person). This is particularly true of instructions. For example:

Change: Anyone wishing to receive a free subscription should enclose payment with his order. (third person)

to: If you wish to receive a free subscription, enclose payment with your order. (second person)

Change: When a man's friends begin to flatter him on how young he looks, it's a sure sign he's getting old.

to: When your friends begin to flatter you on how young you look, it's a sure sign you're getting old.— *Mark Twain*

Revise to eliminate masculine pronouns. This is frequently the best solution to getting bogged down with pronouns. The variety of ways we can express ourselves makes rewriting a relatively simple matter.

The tennis player must practice his serve . . .
The tennis player must practice serving . . .

The child who is afraid to go to bed by himself . . .
The child who is afraid to go to bed alone . . .

An economist is an expert who will know tomorrow why the things he predicted yesterday didn't happen today.
— *Laurence J. Peter*

An economist is an expert who will know tomorrow why yesterday's predictions didn't happen today.

The consumer can stretch disposable income if he refrains from impulse buying.
The consumer can stretch disposable income by refraining from impulse buying.

Job Titles and Descriptions

When men filled most of the jobs outside of the home and women's work was largely inside it, job titles incorporating the suffix -*man* were appropriate. In today's job market where few positions remain strictly male territory, continued use of words that incorporate -*man* produces an inhibitory effect that may discourage female applicants. Similarly, job titles ending in -*ess* and -*ette* may discourage male applicants or offend female applicants.

Recognizing this potential for discrimination, the U.S. Department of Labor has revised its system of occupational classification. The following examples from their *Job Title Revisions* indicate the flavor of the changes.

Former Wording	Revised Wording
airline steward, stewardess	flight attendant
cameraman	camera operator
draftsman	drafter
forelady, foreman	supervisor
lineman	line installer, line repairer
maid	house worker
salesman	sales agent, sales associate
seamstress	sewer, mender
watchman	guard

Some of these revisions seem awkward to us, accustomed as we are to the old ways of expressing ourselves. But if you consider that a word like *salesperson* has been used for years without calling for comment, it may not be too farfetched to suggest that our ears will eventually accept such words as *businessperson* or *spokesperson*.

The suffix -*er* can be a natural substitute for sexually biased terms such as draftsman (e.g., drafter). It has long been used in words like laborer, shopper, photographer, lawyer, runner, and writer. Is it any harder to say "repairer" than "explorer"? Many states have changed the term *workmen's*, as in *workmen's compensation*, to *worker's compensation* to reflect the trend toward neutral words.

Revising to eliminate bias is largely a matter of motivation. The growing number of women in business suggests that you will want to avoid confusing or offending your reader. The fringe benefit you will find is that nonsexist writing helps you communicate clearly and accurately.

7

The Benevolent Dictator

CHAPTER 7

The Benevolent Dictator

Dictation has become an indispensable management skill. Whether you work in a giant corporation or a two-person company, it is to your advantage to master the art of dictating letters.

Dictation is probably the single most effective means of reducing the cost of labor in an office. Even the novice can save time by dictating instead of writing longhand. The time spent in transcription is also decreased, especially if you use dictating equipment and word processors.

But these savings will be diminished if the dictator fails to prepare his or her material adequately; unnecessary rewrites are a waste of time. And typing speed means little if the typist must spend valuable time listening to a mumbled passage again and again, trying to discern the words.

Read the instructions supplied by the manufacturer of your dictating equipment. This is an obvious first step, but many people skip it. Though instructions can be tedious and poorly written, they often reveal the less obvious features and conveniences of the machinery.

When dictating a letter, keep in mind that between you and the desired letter is a person with hearing and mind-reading capabilities no greater than your own. Computers that enhance your voice and screen out "noise" may one day replace all such human intermediaries. But for the present, whether you dictate to a machine or a person, the words you dictate will be heard by human ears and transmitted by human fingers to a typewriter or word processor. Remember that!

The following guidelines for improving your dictating skills are written on the assumption that you will be using dictating equipment. However, the suggestions apply, for the most part, even if you are dictating directly to your secretary.

These dictation guidelines will help you complete more correspondence in less time and with fewer rewrites than you thought possible. Once mastered, dictation can be used in writing longer documents, such as reports and proposals.

Advantages of Person-to-Person Dictation

- Twice as fast as longhand.
- Secretary can help compose letters; serve as a sounding board for ideas; remind you of dates and facts.
- Confidential material can be handled with greater security.

Advantages of Machine Dictation

- Four times as fast as longhand.
- Dictator can dictate whenever and wherever the need arises, without depending on the availability of another person.
- Secretary's time is not tied up during dictation.
- Dictator can use spots of previously wasted time for routine dictation.
- Transcription is faster, more reliable; eliminates the problem of being unable to read shorthand notes after the passage of time.
- Transcription can be done by any typist, not just the person who wrote the shorthand.
- More compatible with a word processing center; makes most efficient use of personnel.

Preliminaries

Arrange a comfortable work area.

You will need:

> Ample desk or table space
>
> A comfortable chair
>
> Good lighting
>
> Quiet

Eliminate distracting noises; background music may soothe your nerves, but it's not apt to have the same effect on the typist who must strain to hear your voice over it. If you dictate at home, do it away from children, dogs, and television sets.

Place the dictating equipment within easy reach, with no extension cord to trip over (in case you like to think on your feet).

Collect reference materials.

Reference materials might include:

Previous correspondence

Notes from a meeting

Addresses and phone numbers

Prices

Material to be enclosed

Arrange these items in the order in which you will refer to them. Doing so helps organize your thinking and avoids interruptions to search for some piece of information once you have started dictating.

Read each letter to be answered.

Make notes in the margins or underline if you want to respond to a particular statement. If a decision is involved, make it—or find the right person to do so.

Work from an outline.

An outline forces you to think. What is your purpose in writing the letter? Your outline will show how you plan to accomplish it.

List the subjects to be covered. You can determine their sequence later and number them accordingly; at first, just write down the topics to make sure that nothing is omitted. As appropriate, add supporting or related details for each topic. A few key words will probably be all you need. The goal is to remind yourself of the subjects you want to cover and to allow you to organize them most effectively before they are typed.

See Chapter 2, *Composing a Better Letter,* for a more complete discussion of outlining.

Handle letters only once, whenever possible.

As you read the day's mail, dictate your reply to any letter that only requires a simple answer. This will clear the decks for the more complicated responses and save the time lost in multiple handling of the mail.

A Word to the Novice

When you are ready to start dictating, you may find that you have a rapid pulse, sweaty palms, and a self-consciousness that paralyzes your thoughts. The cure for this form of mike fright is to select an easy letter and plunge right in. Remember that the best dictator is not necessarily the most fluent, but rather the one who is best organized.

You don't have to speak continuously once you begin, so pause as often as necessary to regroup. Furthermore, you can make corrections easily. After all, your words have not been etched in stone but merely captured on tape. They can be altered as easily as they were put there in the first place.

Don't worry about dictating perfect copy. If you know a letter will need revising, tell the typist in your opening instructions that this is to be a rough draft. This will signal the typist not to waste effort in bringing the letter to the standards of final typed copy. Get your ideas out even if you have to leave some gaps or use a word that you know is not quite right. Some people need to see their words on paper before they hit upon a better way to express an idea.

You may find it helpful to practice dictating from a letter that has already been typed. Select a letter from your files that would be typical of your correspondence. Dictate both the instructions and text that the typist would need in order to duplicate the letter. Any differences will show where you need to improve your dictating technique — or talk to your typist to clear up misunderstandings.

An example of a practice tape might be as follows:

> "Operator, this letter is to be typed in final form on company letterhead using Full Block style. The letter is addressed to Ms. Sarah Grober, S as in Sam, a-r-a-h, Capital G as in Golf, r-o-b as in Boy, e-r, next line Fidelity Associates Comma I-n-c Period, next line 540 Business Center Drive Comma Suite 475, next line Dallas Comma Texas 74590 Paragraph Dear Ms. Grober Colon Paragraph . . ." and so on.

Be sure to give adequate closing instructions as well. For example:

> "Sign the letter Sincerely yours Comma Alice T. James, next line Personnel Manager. Operator, indicate an enclosure and send the attached application form with the letter. Thank you—that's the last letter on this tape."

Most of the differences between a novice and an experienced dictator disappear after only a few hours of practice. As you gain experience, the awkwardness you feel will diminish. Your focus will shift from the mechanics to the material being composed, from *how* you are saying something to *what* you are saying.

Dictating Technique

When dictating, you are speaking to two individuals: the typist and the recipient of the letter. It is important to develop a style that tells the typist whether you are dictating instructions or actual text. The easiest way to distinguish between them is to preface all instructions with the typist's name, when you know it. If the tape goes to a word processing center or typing pool, use a term such as *Operator* or *Typist*. This warns the individual not to type the instructions that follow.

Identify yourself by name, department, or whatever information is needed when the typist transcribes for more than one individual.

Describe the material (e.g., letter, memo), estimate its probable length, indicate if it is a rough draft, and give any special instructions:

- letter format, if different from company standard
- number of copies
- distribution
- type of stationery
- priority of the item
- mailing instructions (e.g., registered, Express Mail, confidential)

Speak distinctly.

Enunciate word endings and small words clearly; they are often crucial to your meaning. "Not" is an example of a crucial small word. Keep the volume of your voice even, and choose a speed at which you are comfortable.

Avoid distracting mannerisms.

Throat clearing, placing your hand over the microphone, chewing gum, eating, smoking, jingling coins or keys, pressing the dictate button without speaking, or starting to speak as you turn the machine on so that part of your words are lost, will all diminish your effectiveness as a dictator. Being considerate of your secretary/typist pays dividends in increased productivity.

Give adequate instructions as you dictate.

Most instructions must precede the part of the letter to which they apply.

- Indicate special format (such as indented material with bullets), change of spacing, or underlining.
- Spell unusual proper names, foreign or technical words.
- Spell sound-alikes (sight, cite, site).
  Note: When dictating sound-alike letters *(f* and *s, m* and *n, b* and *p)*, say "F as in Frank," and so on.
- Indicate capital letters before you say the word you want capitalized ("Operator, the following word is all caps," or "Operator, use initial caps on the following three words, please").
- Specify how you want numbers written ($10,000,000, $10 million dollars, or ten million dollars).
- Indicate paragraphs; you have a better sense of the letter as a whole and its natural break points than does a typist who is hearing each sentence for the first time without knowing what follows.
- Dictate routine punctuation if you wish, but always indicate quotation marks, colons, and semicolons.

Proper punctuation is essential to the meaning of your letter. If you are comfortable dictating commas and periods, do so; but if you have a typist who has a better grasp of punctuation than you do, omit commas and periods. If neither you nor your typist is competent in this area, keep a handbook such as *Write Right!* nearby.

- Dictate the complimentary close, unless the typist knows your preference.
- Dictate any enclosure lines, recipients of carbon copies, and similar material that follows the signature.
- Indicate when you have completed a letter and when a letter is the last one on the tape.

STOP when you have said what you intended to say.

The tendency to ramble or become hypnotized by the sound of your voice is one of the hazards of dictation. Like the car engine that keeps turning over after you've shut off the ignition, you build up momentum when dictating a letter that can easily carry you past your carefully prepared outline, and past the point where the letter should end.

Watch for the warning signs: repeating yourself unnecessarily, wandering off into marginally important points, using empty phrases. Develop a sense of when you have accomplished your purpose in writing the letter, and then draw it to a close.

Edit carefully.

Spoken words often produce a different effect when they are written. The emphasis your voice gives certain words as you dictate does not appear when the words are transcribed, and your meaning may be lost. Or you may find that three sentences start with *however*— something you hadn't realized till seeing your dictated words on paper.

Editing to correct such faults is an essential part of the writing process; it provides the final polish for your letter. Malcolm Forbes, editor of *Forbes* magazine, demonstrated how to edit in the following passage:

> Somebody ~~has~~ said that words are a lot like inflated money — the more ~~of them that~~ you use, the less each one ~~of them~~ is worth. ~~Right on.~~ Go through your entire letter ~~just~~ as many times as it takes. ~~Search out and~~ Annihilate all unnecessary words, ~~and~~ sentences — even ~~entire~~ paragraphs.

Dictator's Block

Occasionally, words won't flow and ideas refuse to line up in logical order. Here are some suggestions to help jog you off "dead center."

Dictate in shorter spurts.

You may be building up a mental block because your dictating sessions are too long. Try smaller units, giving yourself a change of pace between sessions.

Saturate yourself with relevant information.

Do your homework before actual dictating begins by drawing together germinal ideas that relate to a particular problem. During this brainstorming stage, suspend judgment about how relevant an idea might be — then edit later. Use the five W's of the journalist (who, what, why, when, and where) to probe what you know or can find out about your subject. Read reports or articles that might contribute ideas or stimulate your thinking.

Give your mind time to work.

Faced with a particularly difficult or important letter, start thinking about it days in advance. Give your subconscious a chance to come up with a good approach or the best grouping of ideas. You may want to jot down phrases or key ideas to focus your thinking, but then just let your mind roam over the subject of the letter at odd moments. When you are ready to dictate, you will frequently find that your subconcious has produced just the solution you need.

Consciously reduce stress.

Become aware of areas of your body that are tense. Relax them. Stretch and take deep breaths periodically to keep an adequate flow of oxygen to your brain. Ideas often come more freely when you take simple steps to relieve physical strain.

Don't worry about perfection.

Revising the draft of an important letter is a good investment of time — yours and your typist's. With a word processor, the typist's revision time will be minimal. Using phrasing that doesn't quite suit you, or leaving gaps in your first draft in order to get your ideas on the page, may be more productive in the long run than straining for perfect copy on the first pass at a difficult letter.

Visualize the recipient of the letter.

Seeing the reader in your mind's eye will encourage you to dictate as if you were speaking to the person. Doing so may limber up your thoughts and improve the tone of your letter as well.